WeightWatchers®
ProPoints®
Plan

20 Minute Meals

All recipes **10 ProPoints**® values or under

Sue Ashworth

SIMON &
SCHUSTER
ILLUSTRATED

London · New York · Sydney · Toronto · New Delhi

A CBS COMPANY

First published in Great Britain by
Simon & Schuster UK Ltd, 2013
A CBS Company

Copyright © 2013, Weight Watchers International, Inc.

SIMON AND SCHUSTER
ILLUSTRATED BOOKS
Simon & Schuster UK
222 Gray's Inn Road
London WC1X 8HB
www.simonandschuster.co.uk

10 9 8 7 6 5 4 3 2 1

Weight Watchers, **ProPoints** and the **ProPoints** icon
are the registered trademarks of Weight Watchers
International Inc. and used under license by
Weight Watchers (UK) Ltd. All rights reserved.

Weight Watchers Publications Team: Lucy Clements,
Imogen Prescott, Nina McKerlie
Photography: Steve Baxter
Food preparation: Sue Ashworth
Prop styling: Jenny Iggleden

For Simon & Schuster Illustrated
Director of Illustrated Publishing: Ami Richards
Senior Commissioning Editor: Nicky Hill
Art Director: Corinna Farrow
Production Manager: Katherine Thornton

Colour Reproduction by Dot Gradations Ltd, UK
Printed and bound in Italy

A CIP catalogue for this book is available from
the British Library

ISBN: 978-1-47113-015-1

Pictured on front cover: Quick Beef Bolognese, page 56
Pictured on back cover from left to right: Parma Rostis,
page 32; Garlic Bread Steak with Horseradish Sauce,
page 52; Tortilla Pizzas, page 106; Fresh Fruit Skewers
with Hot Chocolate Sauce, page 132
Pictured on front flap: Giant Couscous Salad, page 98
Pictured on back flap: Keralan Fish Curry, page 80

ProPoints ® value logo: You'll find this easy to read
ProPoints value logo on every recipe throughout this book.
The logo represents the number of **ProPoints** values per serving each
recipe contains. It is not an indication of the fillingness of a recipe.

Weight Watchers **ProPoints** Weight Loss System is a simple way to lose
weight. As part of the Weight Watchers **ProPoints** plan you'll enjoy eating
delicious, healthy, filling foods that help to keep you feeling satisfied for
longer and in control of your portions.

Filling & Healthy Foods are highlighted in green. Focus on these foods
where you can – they are healthy choices that will help you to feel satisfied
for longer.

This symbol denotes a vegetarian recipe and assumes that, where
relevant, free range eggs, vegetarian cheese, vegetarian virtually
fat-free fromage frais, vegetarian low fat crème fraîche and vegetarian low
fat yogurts are used. Virtually fat-free fromage frais, low fat crème fraîche
and low fat yogurts may contain traces of gelatine so they are not always
vegetarian. Please check the labels.

This symbol denotes a dish that can be frozen. Unless otherwise
stated, you can freeze the finished dish for up to 1 month. Defrost
thoroughly and reheat until the dish is piping hot throughout.

Recipe notes

Egg size: medium unless otherwise stated.
Raw eggs: only the freshest eggs should be used. Pregnant women, the
elderly and children should avoid recipes with eggs which are not fully
cooked or raw.
All fruits and vegetables: medium size unless otherwise stated.
Chocolate: use chocolate with a minimum of 70% cocoa solids.
Low fat spread: where a recipe states to use a low fat spread, a light
spread with a fat content of no less than 38% should be used.
Stock: stock cubes should be used in the recipes, unless otherwise
stated. Prepare them according to the packet instructions, unless directed
otherwise.
Microwaves: microwave timings are for an 850 watt microwave oven.
Cooking times: these are approximate and meant to be guidelines.
Low fat soft cheese: where a recipe states to use low fat soft cheese, a
soft cheese with a fat content of less than 5% should be used.

20 Minute Meals

Contents

Get ready to be fast!

Welcome to the Weight Watchers way of putting good food on the table — FAST.

All the super-quick recipes are designed to help you create delicious, satisfying food that will work within the ProPoints plan to help you lose weight — and keep it off.

20 minutes: it's not

long – yet it *is* long enough to create a mouth-watering meal. We're all so busy these days, with many demands on our time, yet it's great to know that you can still cook proper food, from scratch, that tastes really good – and is good for you, too. These recipes give you the tips, tricks and techniques to cook delicious, filling food in a fuss-free, user-friendly way. Here's how.

Before you begin – get organised

First and foremost, give your kitchen the once-over. Refresh your cupboards, clearing out ingredients that are past their best. Rationalise the space and sort out cans, bottles and packets in a sensible way, so that they are easy to see. Give your fridge and freezer a thorough going over, and start by planning to use ingredients that you already have in stock.

Cast a critical eye over your kitchen equipment and take any complicated gadgets that you never use to the charity shop. But not your food processor or blender – dust them down as they are there to be used in this book and you'll find it hard to live without them. Clear away any unnecessary items from your worktops, to maximise your available space.

It's no problem if you don't have a food processor, you can still make the recipes, it's just that they will take a few minutes longer. One of the handiest gadgets to have is a hand-held blender – inexpensive to buy, and worth every penny. Often they come with added attachments for blending small quantities. And do make sure that your basic equipment is up to speed. A good cook's knife does a multitude of jobs – and is well worth the investment. Also, make sure you have an efficient speed-peeler and garlic crusher. You don't have to spend a fortune – but just think how often this equipment will be used to help you cook efficiently.

On your marks

When you've chosen a recipe and bought the ingredients, read it through a couple of times so that you get the gist of what you'll be doing. It may take a little time to master these recipes and cook them in under 20 minutes, but once you've cooked them a few times it'll be easy to achieve.

Get set

Next, assemble all your ingredients and get out any equipment. At the start of each recipe, there's a handy list of the main utensils needed, to help you get ready. Many recipes ask you to keep the kettle to hand, full of just-boiled water, so that you won't have to wait. Also, to cook foods quickly you need heat – so preheat the grill, oven or saucepans where recommended.

Go!

Once you've started, try not to get distracted. That's not always possible, with the phone ringing, the kids asking questions, and all the other goings-on that typically happen in the kitchen. Ideally, though, try to stick to the cooking times and bear in mind that the recipes have been written to make the best use of your time; for instance, while the pasta is cooking you might be chopping the vegetables for the accompanying sauce. And do tidy up as you go along, to make sure that the decks are clear. On the other hand, if you're not so pressed for time, relax and allow yourself a few more minutes.

Enjoy

Now comes the good bit – sitting down and enjoying the food that you've just cooked. Take note – it's far better to sit and eat slowly, enjoying every mouthful, rather than wolfing down your food at breakneck speed. Put your knife and fork down between mouthfuls, rest a little, and allow your stomach time to realise when it's full. Most of the portion sizes are pretty generous, containing lots of **Filling & Healthy Foods**, which can help you stay fuller for longer.

Planned with *ProPoints* values

Whichever recipes you choose, the *ProPoints* values will have already been calculated, making it easy for you to track. This unique, flexible system enables you to plan and prepare the meals that suit your lifestyle, whether you're cooking for yourself, your family or friends – fitting in with all the demands of a normal, hectic life.

20 Minute Meals Essentials for speedy cooking

Essential tools for speedy cooking

Small equipment

Digital scales (ideally Weight Watchers)
Measuring spoons
Measuring jug
Cook's knife – and keep it sharp
Knife sharpener – use it often
Kitchen scissors – sharp ones
Oil mister for calorie controlled cooking spray
Serrated knife
Small sharp knife
Bread knife
Set of chopping boards in different sizes
Sieves – small and large
Colander
Grater – fine and coarse
Garlic crusher
Speed-peeler

Ladle
Draining spoon
Fish slice
Wooden spoons
Spatula
Masher
Can opener
Rolling pin
Pastry brush
Silicone-coated whisk for all-in-one sauces
Non-stick frying pans – small and large
Non-stick saucepan
Saucepans with lids
Char-grill (griddle) pan
Bamboo sticks
Wok
Mixing bowls
12-hole bun tin

23 cm (9 inch) square shallow cake tin
850 ml (1½ pint) grill-proof serving dish
Large non-stick baking sheet (with sides) or Swiss roll tin
2 large baking sheets
Roasting tin
Wire cooling rack
4 ramekins or heatproof dishes
Foil, non-stick baking paper, kitchen paper, paper bun cases, cling film, freezer bags

Electrical equipment

Kettle
Toaster
Food processor with attachments
Blender
Hand-held blender
Hand-held electric whisk

Handy-to-have ingredients

Herbs and spices

Dried mixed herbs
Cumin seeds
Cajun spice
Chinese five spice powder
Ground mixed spice
Dried curry leaves
Dried chilli flakes
Paprika

Bottles, jars, tubs and tubes

Calorie controlled cooking spray
Olive oil
Tomato purée
Garlic paste
Ginger paste
Lemongrass paste
Thai curry paste
Pesto sauce

Vegetable stock powder
Chicken stock powder
Miso stock powder
A jar of red peppers in brine
Fish sauce
Soy sauce
Olives
Capers
Gravy granules

Storecupboard

Dried pasta – spaghetti, linguine, tagliatelle, farfalle, penne
Couscous – regular and giant
Rice – long grain, basmati, jasmine
Noodles – egg noodles and rice noodles
Canned tuna in brine
Canned tomatoes

Canned beans
Canned vegetables
Reduced fat coconut milk
Soft flour tortillas
Dried cranberries
Dried apricots
Raisins
Porridge oats

Fridge

Reduced fat hard cheese
Low fat soft cheese
Low fat plain yogurt

Freezer

Frozen vegetables – especially peas, carrots and swede
Frozen fish, prawns, fish pie mix
Frozen filo pastry

Soups	Pork, Lamb + Beef	Chicken + Turkey	Fish + Seafood	Vegetarian	Snacks, Desserts + Fruit

Quick ProPoints values index

Carrot and courgette soup 16

Butternut blitz 18

Easy Chinese soup 20

Fabulous fruit combos 140

Super-quick V8 soup 22

Velvety super-greens soup 24

Marvellous mushroom soup 26

Hot raspberry and mango meringues 136

White bean and red pepper dip 122

Banapple muffins 128

Light-as-air lemon soufflé omelettes 134

Vietnamese Pho Bo 28

Saturday morning BMT 38

Cajun turkey salad 72

Peach and plum grills 120

Fruity flapjack squares 126

Fresh fruit skewers with hot chocolate drizzle 132

Spicy bubble and squeak 40

Quorn tikka salad 102

Cottage cheese crunch 120

Peanut butter, banana and chocolate toast 120

Quickie fruit crumble 130

Grape brûlée 138

Smoked haddock Florentine 82

My Thai fish 86

Veggie filo tart 100

Tortilla pizzas
106

Get-up-and-go
granola **124**

Bangers with root
veg mash **36**

Speedy chicken
club **66**

Stuffed mega-
mushrooms **104**

Tex-Mex omelette
burritos **110**

Frittata to go
116

Parma rostis
32

Ultimate Weight
Watchers burger **54**

Veggie chilli with
baked tortilla chips
and carrot salsa **108**

Mediterranean chilli
tomato tagliatelle
114

Pear, Stilton and
walnut melt **120**

Garlic bread steak
with horseradish
sauce **52**

Fragrant Thai chicken
70

Giant couscous
salad **98**

Steak 'n' sides
50

Classic chicken
Caesar **64**

Easy peasy pasta
112

Speedy spaghetti
carbonara **34**

Pork fillet with lemon
and thyme **42**

Minted lamb and
mash **44**

Spicy lamb naan
46

Beef teriyaki and
noodles **48**

Quick beef
bolognese **56**

Chicken jambalaya
60

Chicken pesto pasta
62

Quick chicken pasta
68

Summer vegetable
and turkey linguine
74

Superfast turkey
meatballs **76**

Keralan fish curry
80

Salmon kachumber
84

Seared tuna Niçoise
88

Topsy-turvy fish
pie **90**

Far-flung prawns
92

Fish lovers' sweet
and sour **94**

"I always have tinned chopped tomatoes in my cupboard – not only are they zero ProPoints but they are always handy for soups, chillies, pasta sauces, curries and stews."

Cath Magee Weight Watchers member

Soups

Carrot and courgette soup

An ideal soup to have on standby – in the fridge or the freezer – for a filling snack or light supper. And the good news is one bowl won't add any **ProPoints** values to your daily total.

ProPoints values per serving	
ProPoints values per recipe	2
Serves 4	

At the ready

a kettle of boiling water

a large measuring jug

a large saucepan on the hob

a food processor with grater attachment
(optional)

Ingredients

4 teaspoons vegetable stock powder
(or 1½ vegetable stock cubes)

400 g can chopped tomatoes

2 tablespoons tomato purée

1 teaspoon dried oregano or Italian
mixed herbs

¼ teaspoon dried chilli flakes (optional)

2 large carrots

1 large red onion**, halved**

1 courgette

salt and freshly ground black pepper

1 Measure 850 ml (1½ pints) of boiling water from the kettle into the saucepan and add the vegetable stock powder or cubes, canned tomatoes, tomato purée, dried herbs and chilli flakes (if using). Bring to a rolling boil.

2 Grate the carrots and half the onion in the food processor and transfer to the saucepan. If you don't have a food processor, grate the vegetables with a hand-held grater. Turn down the heat to a simmer.

3 Finely chop the remaining red onion and the courgette. Tip the onion and courgette into the saucepan; partially cover the pan and cook for 12-15 minutes.

4 Check the seasoning then ladle into warm bowls and serve.

Cook's tips
If you prefer a smooth soup, purée it with a hand-held blender, or return the soup to the rinsed-out food processor and blend with the standard chopping blade until smooth.

Use economy chopped canned tomatoes rather than premium ones – they're perfect in this soup.

Freezing suggestion
Why not portion the soup in 'pour and store' bags so that you can freeze it? Take one to work and it will be thawed by lunchtime, ready for reheating in the microwave.

Butternut blitz

Grating the vegetables in your food processor helps them cook more quickly, which means you'll get this soup on the table in double-quick time.

ProPoints values per serving	
ProPoints values per recipe	**1**
Serves 4	

At the ready

- **a kettle of boiling water**
- **a large measuring jug**
- **a large saucepan on the hob**
- **a food processor with grater attachment (optional)**
- **a hand-held blender**

Ingredients

4 teaspoons vegetable stock powder (or 1½ vegetable stock cubes)

600 g (1 lb 5 oz) butternut squash

1 large red pepper

1 large onion

a few drops of balsamic vinegar

salt and freshly ground black pepper

fresh flat leaf parsley **or** basil**, to garnish**

1 Measure 850 ml (1½ pints) of boiling water from the kettle into the saucepan and add the vegetable stock powder or cubes. Put on a low heat.

2 Peel and de-seed the butternut squash. Halve the red pepper and remove the seeds. Cut the squash, pepper and onion into pieces that will fit through the feeder tube on your processor. Reserve a little pepper for the garnish. Grate the vegetables and add them to the saucepan of simmering stock. If you don't have a food processor, chop the vegetables into small pieces.

3 Bring the soup to the boil, then reduce the heat. Partially cover the saucepan and simmer, stirring occasionally, for 15 minutes. Remove from the heat and blend with a hand-held blender until smooth. Season to taste and add a few drops of balsamic vinegar.

4 Ladle into warm bowls and serve at once garnished with a sprinkling of black pepper, the remaining red pepper, cut into thin strips, and flat leaf parsley or basil.

> *Cook's tip* **This soup is lovely if you stir 1 tablespoon of low fat soft cheese through each bowlful, adding 1 *ProPoints* value per serving.**
>
> *To freeze* **Cool the soup quickly, pack it into suitable containers and freeze for up to 3 months.**
>
> *Serving for a special meal?* **Swirl 1 tablespoon of** low fat plain yogurt **on top of each portion for a *ProPoints* value of 1 per serving.**

Easy Chinese soup

Ready-prepared stir-fry vegetables are used to make this super-speedy soup, with its distinctive Asian flavour. Why not make some on a Friday night, and follow with Fish Lovers' Sweet and Sour (see page 94) for your own home-cooked Chinese take-away?

ProPoints values per serving	
ProPoints values per recipe	1
Serves 4	

At the ready

a kettle of boiling water

a large measuring jug

a large saucepan on the hob

Ingredients

4 teaspoons vegetable stock powder (or 1½ vegetable stock cubes)

½ teaspoon Chinese five spice powder

1 teaspoon finely grated fresh root ginger **(or 1 teaspoon ginger paste)**

½ fresh red or green chilli, **de-seeded and thinly sliced (optional)**

350 g pack fresh stir-fry vegetables with beansprouts

1 teaspoon soy sauce

freshly ground black pepper

1 Measure 850 ml (1½ pints) of boiling water from the kettle into the saucepan. Stir in the stock powder or stock cubes and add the Chinese five spice powder, ginger and chilli (if using).

2 Add the bag of stir-fry vegetables. Bring to the boil, then reduce the heat and simmer for 5 minutes. Season with soy sauce and black pepper before serving.

Variation

Try adding 50 g (1¾ oz) cooked, peeled **prawns** or skinless roast chicken to each portion. This will add 1 **ProPoints** value per serving for prawns, and 3 **ProPoints** values per serving for chicken. To keep the soup vegetarian, add 75 g (2¾ oz) chopped silken **tofu** per portion for 2 **ProPoints** values per serving.

Feeling extra hungry? Add 2 x 50 g (1¾ oz)

nests of dried fine egg noodles to the saucepan before adding the vegetables – they will cook in 5 minutes, and will add 3 *ProPoints* values per serving.

When you have a little more time

Prepare the vegetables yourself. Choose from broccoli florets, cauliflower, peppers, mangetout, carrots, spring onions, leeks and beansprouts.

Super-quick V8 soup

Serve this warming soup with a wholemeal roll, or warm up a pitta or Weight Watchers naan bread – though don't forget to add the extra **ProPoints** values. Keep a carton of V8 in your storecupboard for times when you need to rustle something up quickly.

ProPoints values per serving	
ProPoints values per recipe	**6**
Serves 6	

At the ready

a kettle of boiling water

a large measuring jug

a large saucepan on the hob

Ingredients

3 teaspoons vegetable stock powder
(or 1 vegetable stock cube)

6 spring onions**, finely chopped**

1 litre carton V8 vegetable juice

a few shakes of Tabasco pepper sauce

a few sprigs of fresh chives, coriander,
parsley **or** basil**, plus extra to garnish**

salt and freshly ground black pepper

1 Measure 300 ml (10 fl oz) of boiling water from the kettle into the saucepan. Stir in the stock powder or stock cube and add the spring onions. Bring to the boil, reduce the heat and simmer for 3-4 minutes.

2 Pour in the carton of vegetable juice and add a few shakes of Tabasco sauce. Heat and simmer for 5 minutes.

3 Meanwhile, chop the fresh herbs roughly and add them to the saucepan. Simmer for another 2-3 minutes.

4 Season and serve in warmed bowls, scattered with extra chopped chives, coriander, parsley or basil.

Cook's tip **Try using a 1 litre carton of tomato juice instead of V8 juice, though you may need to add a pinch of caster sugar to help balance the flavour.**

Velvety super-greens soup

Get your vitamins in the most delicious way in this stunning green soup. You could serve it chilled, too, for a summer lunch.

ProPoints values per serving	
ProPoints values per recipe	5
Serves 6	

At the ready

a kettle of boiling water
a large measuring jug
a large saucepan on the hob
a blender or hand-held blender

Ingredients

4 teaspoons vegetable stock powder
    (or 1½ vegetable stock cubes)
300 g (10½ oz) broccoli
a bunch of spring onions
85 g bag watercress
200 g (7 oz) young leaf spinach
100 g (3½ oz) low fat soft cheese
100 ml (3½ fl oz) skimmed milk
freshly ground black pepper

1 Measure 850 ml (1½ pints) of boiling water from the kettle into the saucepan. Stir in the stock powder or stock cubes and bring back to the boil.

2 Break the broccoli directly into the saucepan in small florets. Chop any tough stems into small pieces and add these, too. Chop the spring onions roughly and tip them into the saucepan.

3 Simmer the soup, partially covered, for 10 minutes. Reserve a few sprigs of the watercress and add the rest to the saucepan with the spinach. Cook down for 2-3 minutes, stirring them into the soup. It will look as if there are a lot of leaves at first, but they will soon wilt.

4 Transfer the soup to a blender and add the soft cheese and milk. Blend for 15-20 seconds until smooth. Return to the saucepan and reheat gently. Check the seasoning and serve, garnished with the reserved watercress.

Variation

You could use an **onion**, finely chopped, instead of the spring onions.

Cook's tips The beauty of this soup is its bright green colour and fresh taste, so don't be tempted to cook the spinach for more than 3 minutes.

If using larger leaf spinach, tear off the tougher stems and add these to the saucepan earlier, so that they can cook for a little longer until tender.

Serving for a special meal? To make a swirl on top of each portion of soup, reserve 2 tablespoons of the low fat soft cheese and blend it with 1 tablespoon of skimmed milk until smooth, for the same ProPoints values.

Marvellous mushroom soup

It's packed with flavour, so make this soup one of your easy supper options. It's a great dinner-party starter, too – see Cook's tip (below) for simple tricks to posh it up for just 1 extra *ProPoints* value.

ProPoints values per serving	
ProPoints values per recipe	4
Serves 4	

At the ready

a kettle of boiling water
a large measuring jug
a large saucepan on the hob
a garlic crusher
a blender or hand-held blender

Ingredients

4 teaspoons vegetable stock powder
   (or 1½ vegetable stock cubes)
1 onion
400 g (14 oz) mushrooms, plus
   2 reserved for garnish
1 large garlic clove
a small handful of fresh parsley
75 g (2¾ oz) low fat soft cheese
salt and freshly ground black pepper

1 Measure 850 ml (1½ pints) of boiling water from the kettle into the saucepan. Stir in the stock powder or stock cubes. Finely chop the onion and roughly chop the mushrooms and add to the saucepan. Use a garlic crusher to crush the garlic and add it to the pan. Then add most of the parsley – there's no need to chop it.

2 Bring the soup to the boil, reduce the heat and simmer for 10-12 minutes.

3 Transfer the soup to a blender and add the soft cheese. Blend for 15-20 seconds until smooth. Alternatively, use a hand-held blender to purée the soup.

4 Reheat the soup for 1-2 minutes, adding the reserved mushrooms, thinly sliced. Season to taste, then serve, garnished with chopped parsley and a little extra black pepper.

Variation

Use **fresh coriander** instead of parsley and add a teaspoon of ground coriander to the stock for a warm, spicy flavour.

Cook's tip Look out for economy mushrooms, or buy a bumper pack and make twice the quantity of soup, packing and freezing individual portions to use another day.

For a special occasion Add 2 tablespoons of medium sherry to the soup just before serving, and swirl an extra 2 teaspoons of low fat crème fraîche on top of each bowl. This will add 1 *ProPoints* value per serving.

Vietnamese Pho Bo

A beautiful tasting substantial soup that's a meal in itself – perfect for when you want dinner on the table with minimum fuss.

ProPoints values per serving	
ProPoints values per recipe	**12**
Serves 4	

At the ready

a kettle of boiling water

a large measuring jug

a large saucepan on the hob

a non-stick frying pan

Ingredients

1 beef stock cube

2 tablespoons fish sauce

2 teaspoons lemongrass paste

½ teaspoon ground coriander

½ teaspoon cumin seeds

1 star anise (optional)

1 red or white onion

100 g (3½ oz) mushrooms

1 small red chilli

calorie controlled cooking spray

125 g (4½ oz) rump steak

150 g pack ready-to-wok ribbon noodles

50 g (1¾ oz) green or Savoy cabbage, **finely shredded, or** bean sprouts

1   Measure 1 litre (1¾ pints) of boiling water from the kettle into the saucepan. Crumble in the stock cube and add the fish sauce and lemongrass paste. Add the ground coriander, cumin seeds and star anise (if using) and simmer gently for 5 minutes.

2   Meanwhile, thinly slice the onion, mushrooms and chilli, removing the seeds if you prefer a milder taste. Add the sliced vegetables to the saucepan and continue to cook for 6-7 minutes.

3   At the same time, heat a non-stick frying pan or wok and spray with the cooking spray. Slice the rump steak thinly and add to the pan or wok, stir-frying over a high heat for 2-3 minutes. Turn off the heat and set aside to rest for 2-3 minutes.

4   At this point, add the noodles and cabbage or bean sprouts to the saucepan and heat for 1-2 minutes. Ladle the soup into warm bowls and share the steak between them.

Variation

Use a chicken stock cube and **skinless, boneless chicken breast** instead of rump steak, for a **ProPoints** value of 2 per serving.

Cook's tip You can buy ready-prepared lemongrass paste in tubes or jars. Once opened, keep refrigerated and use within the recommended date on the pack.

Remember Fish sauce is used as a seasoning, so it's unlikely that you'll need to add any salt and pepper.

"Healthy cooking doesn't have to mean flavourless cooking. Herbs, spices, chilli, ginger, garlic, lemon and lime juice, soy sauce and Worcestershire sauce can all pep up plain food and turn it into something you really want to eat."

Marianne Eady Weight Watchers member

Pork, Lamb + Beef

Parma rostis

There's something about Parma ham that turns a dish from plain to posh. This is a great dish for a lazy weekend brunch.

ProPoints values per serving	
ProPoints values per recipe	**15**
Serves 2	

At the ready

a food processor with grater attachment

a clean tea towel

a large non-stick frying pan

egg-poacher or small saucepan

Ingredients

300 g (10½ oz) floury potatoes

1 carrot

1 courgette

1 egg white

calorie controlled cooking spray

2 eggs

2 bunches cherry tomatoes on the vine

75 g pack Parma ham

salt and freshly ground black pepper

1 Peel the potatoes and halve them, if large. Grate them in the food processor with the carrot and courgette. Drain off any excess liquid and tip the vegetables on to the clean tea towel, folding it over the top and pressing down to soak up as much moisture as possible. Lightly beat the egg white and add the vegetables. Season and mix them all together.

2 Heat the frying pan and spray with the cooking spray. Split the mixture into 6 rostis and cook for 3-4 minutes per side, patting them down with a spatula to flatten the tops. Preheat the grill.

3 While the rostis are cooking, poach the eggs in an egg-poacher, or cook in lightly simmering water for 3-4 minutes, until done to your liking. At the same time, grill the cherry tomato bunches for 2-3 minutes.

4 Share the rostis between 2 warmed plates. Top with slices of Parma ham and place a poached egg in the middle of each plate. Season with black pepper and serve with the cherry tomato bunches.

Cook's tips To make the rostis look neater, put a cooking ring into the frying pan and spoon a sixth of the mixture into it, levelling the top with a spoon. Lift the ring and repeat until all the mixture is used.

You need a really good non-stick frying pan to cook the rostis with the minimum amount of added fat. It's worth investing in one – and looking after it.

Speedy spaghetti carbonara

Sort out the family supper – fast – with this no-fuss satisfying dish.

ProPoints values per serving	
ProPoints values per recipe	**38**
Serves 4	

At the ready

a large saucepan

a kettle of boiling water

a non-stick frying pan

a mixing bowl

kitchen scissors

a colander

Ingredients

250 g (9 oz) spaghetti or linguine

a bunch of spring onions

150 g (5½ oz) button mushrooms

calorie controlled cooking spray

1 large garlic clove

200 g (7 oz) low fat soft cheese

1 large egg

150 ml (5 fl oz) skimmed milk

15 g (½ oz) Parmesan cheese, finely grated

a small handful of fresh flat leaf parsley

100 g (3½ oz) lean roast ham

freshly ground black pepper

1 Put the spaghetti or linguine into the saucepan and cover with plenty of boiling water from the kettle. Cook for 8-10 minutes until just tender, or according to the packet instructions.

2 Meanwhile, thinly slice the spring onions and mushrooms. Heat the frying pan and spray it with the cooking spray. Add the spring onions and mushrooms to the frying pan with the peeled, halved garlic clove and cook gently for 5 minutes, until softened. Then discard the garlic clove – it has just been used to give flavour to the finished dish.

3 Beat the soft cheese and egg together in a mixing bowl, then add the skimmed milk and half the Parmesan cheese. Snip in the parsley, using scissors, then season with pepper.

4 Reserve 2 tablespoons of the cooking liquid, then drain the pasta through the colander. Return the pasta to the saucepan with the cooking liquid. Stir in the egg mixture, then add the spring onions and mushrooms. Snip in the roast ham, using scissors. Heat gently for 2-3 minutes, stirring, until the egg mixture has cooked and thickened.

5 Serve sprinkled with the remaining Parmesan cheese.

Variation

Replace the mushrooms with a **courgette**, chopped into small pieces.

Cook's tip **If you love garlic, crush the clove into the spring onions and mushrooms for a more pronounced flavour.**

Bangers with root veg mash

This family favourite with a twist is an ideal weekday supper and surprisingly low in *ProPoints* values for real comfort food.

ProPoints values per serving	**6** ProPoints value
ProPoints values per recipe	25
Serves 4	

At the ready

a large saucepan

a kettle of boiling water

a non-stick frying pan

a measuring jug

kitchen scissors

a colander

Ingredients

500 g bag ready-prepared carrot and swede

500 g (1 lb 2 oz) potatoes

8 Weight Watchers pork sausages

1 large red onion

calorie controlled cooking spray

6 heaped teaspoons gravy granules

a small handful of fresh chives

freshly ground black pepper

1 Preheat the grill to medium-high. Put the prepared carrot and swede into the saucepan, cover with boiling water from the kettle and bring back to the boil. Reduce the heat. Peel and cut the potatoes into small chunks. Add them to the saucepan; then cover and simmer briskly for about 15 minutes, until the vegetables are tender.

2 Meanwhile, arrange the sausages on the grill rack and cook them for 12-15 minutes, turning occasionally until evenly browned.

3 While the sausages are cooking, peel and thinly slice the onion. Spray the non-stick frying pan with the cooking spray and cook the onion for 6-7 minutes, until soft and browned. Measure in 450 ml (16 fl oz) of boiling water from the kettle, then sprinkle in the gravy granules, stirring with a wooden spoon until thickened. Snip the chives into the frying pan, using scissors. Keep warm over a low heat.

4 Drain the vegetables in the colander and return them to the saucepan. Mash thoroughly, season with black pepper and reheat for a few moments. Share between 4 warmed plates and serve 2 sausages each with the red onion gravy. A green vegetable such as cabbage makes an ideal accompaniment.

Variation

For a vegetarian version use Quorn sausages and vegetarian gravy granules.

Cook's tip When time is really tight, use frozen carrot and swede instead of fresh. And when you have more time, peel and chop the carrots and swede from scratch.

Make the meal go further Serve with extra vegetables, such as cabbage, broccoli or cauliflower.

Saturday morning BMT

Enjoy this delicious weekend breakfast of bacon, mushrooms and tomatoes. It's got all the taste you want for a low **ProPoints** value.

ProPoints values per serving	**3** ProPoints value

ProPoints values per recipe	**6**
Serves 2	

At the ready

a non-stick frying pan

a measuring jug

a kettle of boiling water

Ingredients

150 g (5½ oz) mushrooms

1 teaspoon vegetable stock powder

4 trimmed bacon medallions

2 tomatoes

2 slices Weight Watchers Thick Sliced Wholemeal Loaf

freshly ground black pepper

1 Preheat the grill. Slice the mushrooms and put them into the non-stick frying pan. Measure 200 ml (7 fl oz) boiling water from the kettle and add the stock powder. Add the stock to the frying pan and simmer the mushrooms for 6-7 minutes.

2 Meanwhile, arrange the bacon medallions on the grill rack and cook for 2-3 minutes; then turn them over. Slice the tomatoes thickly and arrange them next to the bacon. Grill for another 2-3 minutes.

3 At the same time, toast the slices of bread. Place the toast on 2 warmed plates. Drain the mushrooms and arrange them on or next to the toast, along with the tomatoes and bacon. Season with black pepper and serve.

> **Cook's tip** **Use trimmed back bacon rashers if you can't find bacon medallions; the *ProPoints* values will be 5 per serving.**
>
> **For a sandwich** **Use 2 slices of Weight Watchers Malted Danish Loaf per person instead of the wholemeal bread. The *ProPoints* values will be 4 per serving.**

Spicy bubble and squeak

Make this spicy version of a classic for a weekend brunch – it's the sort of dish teenagers love, too.

ProPoints values per serving	**4** ProPoints value
ProPoints values per recipe	**18**
Serves 4	

At the ready

a large saucepan
a kettle of boiling water
a large non-stick frying pan or wok
a colander
kitchen scissors

Ingredients

500 g (1 lb 2 oz) potatoes
1 large red onion
calorie controlled cooking spray
300 g (10½ oz) Savoy or green cabbage
1 green chilli
1 teaspoon cumin seeds
250g (9 oz) lean roast ham
a small handful of fresh coriander,
**   reserving a few sprigs for garnish**
salt and freshly ground black pepper

1 Peel and cut the potatoes into small chunks. Add them to the saucepan; cover with boiling water from the kettle and simmer briskly for 6-8 minutes, until just tender.

2 Meanwhile, peel and thinly slice the onion. Spray the non-stick frying pan or wok with the cooking spray and cook the onion for 3-4 minutes, until softened. While it's cooking, finely shred the cabbage; add it to the pan with the onion and stir-fry for 3-4 minutes, until the cabbage is wilted.

3 Drain the potatoes in the colander, letting them steam-dry for 1-2 minutes.

4 While the potatoes are draining, thinly slice the chilli, removing the seeds. Add the chilli to the frying pan or wok with the cumin seeds. Add the potatoes; then snip in the ham and the coriander with a pair of scissors. Stir-fry everything together for 3-4 minutes, adding an extra couple of sprays of the cooking spray.

5 Check the seasoning before piling the bubble and squeak on to warmed plates and serve with extra sprigs of coriander.

Variation

Try topped with poached **eggs**. Just cook 4 medium eggs in an egg-poacher, or cook in gently simmering water, during the final 4-5 minutes of cooking time. This will add 2 **ProPoints** values per serving.

> **Cook's tip** **This is a great recipe for using up leftover boiled potatoes.**

Pork fillet with lemon and thyme

Pork fillet is tender and delicious – perfect for this just-got-home-from-work dish.

ProPoints values per serving

10
ProPoints value

ProPoints values per recipe	**40**
Serves 4	

At the ready

- **a fine grater**
- **a large saucepan**
- **a kettle of boiling water**
- **a large non-stick frying pan**
- **a measuring jug**
- **a colander**

Ingredients

- **1 tablespoon dried thyme**
- **1 tablespoon plain flour**
- **1 lemon**
- **400 g (14 oz) pork fillet, in one piece**
- **225 g (8 oz) jasmine or basmati rice**
- **calorie controlled cooking spray**
- **2 teaspoons vegetable or chicken stock powder (or 1 stock cube)**
- **250 g (9 oz) button mushrooms**
- **6 spring onions**
- **200 g (7 oz) broccoli**
- **75 g (2¾ oz) frozen peas**
- **salt and freshly ground black pepper**

1. Sprinkle the dried thyme and flour on to a large plate. Finely grate the zest from the lemon on to the plate, then season. Mix the seasoned flour together and roll the whole pork fillet in the mixture. Cut the fillet into 1 cm (½ inch) slices.

2. Put the rice into the saucepan and cover with plenty of boiling water from the kettle. Cook for 8 minutes. Re-fill the kettle and boil it.

3. Meanwhile, heat the frying pan and spray with the cooking spray. Add the pork slices and cook over a high heat for 2 minutes, then turn over and cook on the other side for 2 minutes, until browned.

4. Measure 200 ml (7 fl oz) boiling water from the kettle and stir in the stock powder or cube. Halve or slice the mushrooms and add them to the frying pan with the stock. Reduce the heat and simmer for 5 minutes.

5. While the pork is cooking, finely slice the spring onions and break the broccoli into small florets. Add them to the rice when it has been cooking for 8 minutes, along with the frozen peas. Cook for 3-4 minutes more, until the vegetables are tender.

6. Drain the rice and vegetables through the colander and share them between 4 warmed plates. Serve the pork and mushrooms on top of the rice. Slice the lemon into wedges and serve as a garnish, if liked.

Variation

Try using **skinless, boneless chicken breast** in place of the pork fillet, for a **ProPoints** value of 9 per serving.

Cook's tip **You can use dried mixed herbs or rosemary instead of thyme.**

Minted lamb and mash

Here's how to stretch mash – and your **ProPoints** values – in one easy family recipe.

ProPoints values per serving	**10** ProPoints value
ProPoints values per recipe	39
Serves 4	

At the ready

- **a large saucepan**
- **a kettle of boiling water**
- **a char-grill pan or the grill**
- **a colander**
- **kitchen scissors**

Ingredients

- **450 g (1 lb) potatoes**
- **1 medium cauliflower**
- **100 g (3½ oz) frozen peas**
- **4 x 125 g (4½ oz) lean lamb leg steaks**
- **calorie controlled cooking spray**
- **a small handful of fresh chives or parsley**
- **4 heaped teaspoons gravy granules**
- **1 tablespoon mint sauce**
- **salt and freshly ground black pepper**

1 Peel and cut the potatoes into small chunks. Add them to the saucepan; cover with boiling water from the kettle and simmer briskly for 5 minutes.

2 Meanwhile, break the cauliflower into florets. Add them to the saucepan with the potatoes. Add more boiling water; cover and cook for 10-12 minutes more, adding the frozen peas for the final 2 minutes.

3 At the same time, preheat the char-grill pan or grill. Spray the lamb steaks with the cooking spray, then char-grill or grill them for 3-4 minutes per side. When cooked, cover the steaks with foil and leave to rest in a warm place.

4 Drain the potatoes, cauliflower and peas thoroughly in the colander. Return the vegetables to the saucepan and mash them, snipping in the chives or parsley with a pair of scissors. Season and reheat for a few moments.

5 Make the gravy with the instant gravy granules according to the packet instructions then stir in the mint sauce. Serve with the lamb and mash and a vegetable of your choice such as carrots.

Cook's tips

Serve with extra vegetables, such as carrots, cabbage or broccoli, without adding any more *ProPoints* values.

Fresh mint leaves will turn black if added to the hot mash: that's why this recipe uses chives or parsley for the mash and the mint sauce to flavour the gravy.

Spicy lamb naan

This tasty lamb dish is super-quick and exceptionally tasty – the ideal alternative to a take-away curry.

ProPoints values per serving	10
ProPoints values per recipe	20
Serves 2	

At the ready

**a food processor with slicer and grater
    attachments**
a wok or large non-stick frying pan
kitchen scissors

Ingredients

225 g (8 oz) lean lamb leg steaks
2 tablespoons lemon juice
1 teaspoon ground coriander
½ teaspoon cumin seeds
1 red onion
calorie controlled cooking spray

For the salad

1 large carrot
15 g (½ oz) raisins
1 teaspoon black onion seeds (optional)

For the raita

75 g (2¾ oz) low fat plain yogurt
¼ cucumber
**a few sprigs of fresh mint or coriander,
    reserving a few for garnish**
**2 x 44 g Weight Watchers mini plain naan
    bread**

1 Put the lamb steaks on a board and sprinkle them with the lemon juice, ground coriander and cumin seeds. Slice them thinly and set aside.

2 Slice the red onion in the food processor or by hand. Heat the wok or non-stick frying pan and spray with the cooking spray. Add the onion and cook over a medium-high heat, stirring often, for 2-3 minutes. Add the lamb and continue to cook for 5 more minutes.

3 Meanwhile, fit the grater attachment into the food processor and grate the carrot. Tip it into a serving bowl and add the raisins and black onion seeds, if using.

4 Put the yogurt in a small serving bowl. Grate the cucumber in the food processor; drain it and mix it into the yogurt. Snip in the fresh mint or coriander, using a pair of scissors.

5 Warm the naan bread, either under the grill or in a toaster. Put the naan on 2 plates and top each one with the lamb mixture. Serve with the carrot salad and cucumber raita. Garnish with mint or coriander sprigs.

Cook's tip To save time, make sure that you get all the ingredients out of the fridge and cupboards before you start.

For a delicious variation Try serving the lamb with kachumber, a chilli-spiced Indian salad. You'll find the recipe on page 84, where it is served with a salmon dish.

Beef teriyaki and noodles

If you like eating out at noodle bars, try this simple Japanese-style recipe at home instead.

ProPoints values per serving	**10** ProPoints value
ProPoints values per recipe	**20**
Serves 2	

At the ready

a kettle of boiling water

a wok or large non-stick frying pan

a colander

Ingredients

250 g (9 oz) lean rump steak

2 tablespoons teriyaki marinade

2 x 50 g nests of dried fine egg noodles

a bunch of spring onions

2 celery sticks

200 g (7 oz) sugar snap peas or mangetout

calorie controlled cooking spray

freshly ground black pepper

1 Slice the steak thinly across the grain. Put the strips in a bowl (don't use a metal one) and add the teriyaki marinade, tossing the meat to coat it. Leave to marinate for 10 minutes.

2 Meanwhile, put the nests of noodles into a heatproof bowl and cover with boiling water from the kettle. Set aside for 5 minutes.

3 While the noodles are soaking, thinly slice the spring onions and celery. Halve the sugar snap peas or mangetout.

4 Heat the wok or large non-stick frying pan and spray with the cooking spray. Add the sliced vegetables and stir-fry for 2-3 minutes. Add the drained steak (reserving the marinade) and stir-fry for 2 minutes. Drain the noodles and add to the wok and stir-fry for a few moments to heat through. Add the reserved marinade and season with black pepper. Serve immediately.

Variation

This recipe is also ideal for sliced **turkey breast steaks**, for a **ProPoints** value of 9 per serving.

Steak 'n' sides

For a special occasion cook char-grilled steak for dinner.

ProPoints values per serving

ProPoints values per recipe **18**
Serves 2

At the ready

a large saucepan
a kettle of boiling water
a saucepan
a measuring jug
a char-grill pan or non-stick frying pan

Ingredients

300 g (10½ oz) new potatoes
350 g (12 oz) mushrooms
**2 teaspoons vegetable stock powder
    (or 1 stock cube)**
2 x 150 g (5½ oz) lean fillet steaks
calorie controlled cooking spray
**2 bunches of cherry tomatoes on the
    vine**
salt and freshly ground black pepper

1 Halve or quarter the new potatoes, unless they're really small, so that they cook more quickly. Put them in the large saucepan and cover with boiling water from the kettle. Add a pinch of salt, cover and simmer for 15 minutes, until tender.

2 Meanwhile, slice the mushrooms and put them in the smaller saucepan. Measure in 200 ml (7 fl oz) boiling water from the kettle and add the stock powder or crumble in the stock cube. Heat and simmer gently for 8-10 minutes.

3 When the potatoes have been cooking for 5-6 minutes, preheat the char-grill pan or non-stick frying pan. Spray the steaks with the cooking spray and add them to the pan, cooking for 3-4 minutes per side, or to your liking. When done, remove from the pan and leave to rest, covered with foil.

4 Cook the tomatoes in the char-grill pan or non-stick frying pan for 1-2 minutes while you serve up the rest of the meal. Drain the potatoes and mushrooms and share between warmed plates. Put the steaks alongside and serve with the cherry tomato bunches, seasoned with black pepper.

Variation

If you prefer, use rump or sirloin steak instead of fillet.

Garlic bread steak with horseradish sauce

A classic sandwich for a late supper.

ProPoints values per serving	8
ProPoints values per recipe	32
Serves 4	

At the ready

a garlic crusher
a char-grill pan or non-stick frying pan

Ingredients

100 g (3½ oz) 0% fat Greek yogurt
2 teaspoons horseradish sauce
2 x 15 cm (6 inch) slices French bread
4 teaspoons low fat spread
1 large garlic clove
4 x 75 g (2¾ oz) minute steaks
calorie controlled cooking spray
mixed salad leaves**, to serve**
freshly ground black pepper

1 Preheat the grill. In a bowl mix together the Greek yogurt and horseradish sauce.

2 Slice the French bread in half horizontally, then spread each cut surface with 1 teaspoon of low fat spread. Crush the garlic, and spread a little over each piece, then toast the cut sides until lightly browned.

3 Heat the char-grill pan or frying pan. Spray the steaks with the cooking spray, then add them to the pan and cook over a high heat for 1 minute per side.

4 Pile some salad leaves on the toasted bread; add the steaks and spoon a dollop of the horseradish sauce on top. Season with black pepper.

Variation

You could make this recipe with 4 x 100 g (3½ oz) pieces of bashed-out **skinless, boneless chicken breast** – though cook them for 3-4 minutes per side to make sure they are done. The **ProPoints** values per serving will be 8 .

Feeling famished? Use 1 x 10 cm (4 inch) piece of bread per person, and serve the steaks sandwiched between the bread. The *ProPoints* values per serving will be 9.

Ultimate Weight Watchers burger

The best thing about a home-made burger? You know exactly what's gone into it. Make these for movie night at home on the sofa.

ProPoints values per serving	
ProPoints values per recipe	30
Serves 4	

At the ready

a food processor with grater attachment
kitchen scissors
a char-grill pan or the grill

Ingredients

450 g (1 lb) extra lean minced beef
1 onion
1 large carrot
2 teaspoons mixed dried herbs
a small handful of fresh chives
1 tablespoon Worcestershire sauce
calorie controlled cooking spray
4 standard burger buns
1 Little Gem lettuce
2 tomatoes
4 gherkins
salt and freshly ground black pepper

1 Put the minced beef in a mixing bowl. Roughly chop the onion and carrot; then grate them in the food processor. Mix them into the minced beef with the dried herbs.

2 Snip the chives into the mince mixture, using a pair of scissors. Add the Worcestershire sauce and season. Mix again; then form the mixture into 4 burgers.

3 Heat the char-grill pan or the grill. Spray the burgers with the cooking spray and cook them for 4-5 minutes on each side, or until done to your liking.

4 Meanwhile, slice the burger buns in half and lightly toast the cut sides. Shred the lettuce and pile some on the base of each bun. Place the cooked burgers on the bases. Slice the tomatoes and gherkins and arrange on top. Add the bun lids and serve at once, seasoned with black pepper.

Variation

If you don't eat beef, try using pork or turkey mince instead. Pork burgers will be 9 **ProPoints** values per serving with lean pork mince and 10 with standard pork mince. Turkey burgers will be 8 **ProPoints** values per serving.

Customise your burger Add a processed cheese slice for an additional 2 *ProPoints* values per serving; a grilled rasher of lean back bacon for an additional 2 *ProPoints* values per serving; or crumble 15 g (½ oz) of blue Stilton over the burger for an additional 2 *ProPoints* values per serving.

Quick beef bolognese

Try this speedy version of one of the top ten favourite family meals in the UK. It's just as easy to make a vegetarian version, too – see Cook's tip below.

ProPoints values per serving	
ProPoints values per recipe	**40**
Serves 4	

At the ready

a large heavy-based saucepan

a food processor with grater attachment

a large saucepan

a kettle of boiling water

At the ready

450 g (1 lb) extra lean minced beef

1 onion

1 large carrot

1 large courgette

400 g can chopped tomatoes

2 tablespoons tomato purée

1 tablespoon dried mixed Italian herbs

200 g (7 oz) mushrooms, sliced

250 g (9 oz) quick-cook dried spaghetti

salt and freshly ground black pepper

fresh basil leaves, to garnish (optional)

1 Heat the heavy-based saucepan. Add the mince and let it sear over a high heat; stir after 30-40 seconds and cook for another 3-4 minutes until browned. This step is important to achieve a good flavour.

2 Grate the onion, carrot and courgette in the food processor and add them to the meat.

3 Tip in the tomatoes, add the tomato purée and bring the mixture to the boil. Add the dried herbs and stir the mushrooms into the sauce. Lower the heat slightly and cook for 12-14 minutes.

4 Five minutes before the bolognese sauce is ready, cook the spaghetti in a large saucepan with plenty of boiling water from the kettle. Cook for 4-5 minutes. Drain well, and share the spaghetti between 4 warmed plates.

5 Check the seasoning before spooning the bolognese sauce on top of the spaghetti. Serve at once, garnished with basil leaves, if using.

Variation

Try using turkey mince instead of beef mince. It makes an excellent alternative to red meat – and the **ProPoints** values per serving will be 10.

Cook's tip There is time to cook regular dried spaghetti within 20 minutes: just remember to put it on to cook earlier – it will need 10-12 minutes.

For a vegetarian version Use a 500 g pack of frozen Quorn mince – there's no need to thaw it first. *ProPoints* values per serving will be 9.

"Weigh potatoes then put a cocktail stick in each one and cook with everyone else's – no fiddling when they're cooked as you know which ones are yours!"

Liz Hurrell Weight Watchers member

Chicken + Turkey

Chicken jambalaya

Try this quick and easy Cajun-style recipe when you fancy something spicy.

ProPoints values per serving	
ProPoints values per recipe	40
Serves 4	

At the ready

a large saucepan

a kettle of boiling water

a food processor with slicing attachment

a large non-stick frying pan or wok

a colander

Ingredients

250 g (9 oz) long grain rice

3 sprigs fresh thyme, plus extra to garnish

1 onion

3 celery sticks

1 red pepper

175 g (6 oz) closed cup mushrooms

1 teaspoon vegetable oil

2 teaspoons Cajun seasoning or paprika

½ teaspoon chilli powder

400 g (14 oz) cooked, skinless, boneless chicken breast

4 tomatoes

freshly ground black pepper

1 Put the rice into the saucepan and cover with plenty of boiling water from the kettle. Add the sprigs of thyme; then cover and cook over a medium heat for 12 minutes, or according to the packet instructions, until tender.

2 Meanwhile, use the food processor to slice the onion, celery, red pepper and mushrooms. Heat the oil in the frying pan or wok and tip in the vegetables from the food processor. Stir-fry them for 4-5 minutes.

3 Drain the rice in the colander; then add it to the frying pan and add the Cajun seasoning or paprika and chilli powder.

4 Chop the chicken and tomatoes and add them to the pan. Cook for 2-3 more minutes, stirring constantly until heated through. Check the seasoning, adding some pepper and an extra pinch of Cajun seasoning or chilli powder, if needed.

5 Spoon on to 4 warmed plates and serve at once, garnished with a few thyme sprigs.

Variation

Use 250 g (9 oz) cooked, peeled **prawns** instead of cooked chicken, for a change. This will work out at 8 **ProPoints** values per serving.

Cook's tip Save even more time by preparing the rice ahead, rinsing it with cold water to cool it quickly, then refrigerating until required later in the day. Make sure you reheat it thoroughly.

Chicken pesto pasta

If there's just the two of you then try this chicken pasta dish for dinner – you'll have most of the ingredients in your storecupboard.

ProPoints values per serving	
ProPoints values per recipe	19
Serves 2	

At the ready

a large saucepan
a kettle of boiling water
a non-stick frying pan
a fine grater
a colander
kitchen scissors

Ingredients

125 g (4½ oz) rigatoni or penne
1 red onion
calorie controlled cooking spray
150 g (5½ oz) skinless, boneless chicken breast
1 small lemon
12 cherry tomatoes
2 tablespoons red pesto sauce
6 black or green olives
1 tablespoon capers, drained
a small handful of fresh flat leaf parsley
freshly ground black pepper

1 Put the pasta in the saucepan and cover with plenty of boiling water from the kettle. Cook for 8-10 minutes, or according to the packet instructions.

2 Meanwhile, thinly slice the onion. Heat the frying pan and spray with the cooking spray. Add the onion and cook over a medium heat for 2 minutes while you slice the chicken breast into chunks. Add the chicken to the pan and cook for 5-6 minutes, stirring often. Finely grate the zest from the lemon directly into the frying pan.

3 While the chicken is cooking, halve the tomatoes. Add them to the chicken after it has cooked for 5-6 minutes. Then stir in the pesto sauce, olives and capers. Add about 2 tablespoons of hot water from the kettle and squeeze in the juice from half the lemon. Keep warm over a low heat.

4 Drain the pasta in the colander and return it to the saucepan. Stir in the chicken pesto mixture; then snip in about half the parsley using scissors. Heat for about 1 minute, stirring gently.

5 Share the pasta between warmed plates and snip the rest of the parsley over the top. Season with black pepper and serve with the remaining lemon, cut into wedges, if desired.

Variation

You can use green pesto instead of red, the choice is yours – although remember to add the extra *ProPoints* values.

Cook's tip **Add some extra vegetables if you like, such as chopped** asparagus, green beans **or** courgettes. **Just cook them with the pasta, adding them for the final 3-4 minutes of cooking time. You'll be putting more food on your plate, without adding any extra *ProPoints* values.**

Classic chicken Caesar

This is an ideal version of an old favourite for a summer lunch: the secret is its lighter dressing.

9 ProPoints value

ProPoints values per serving

| ProPoints values per recipe | 17 |
| Serves 2 | |

At the ready

a colander

a mixing bowl

Ingredients

1 Romaine lettuce

1 large garlic clove

50 g (1¾ oz) low fat soft cheese

100 g (3½ oz) low fat plain yogurt

2 teaspoons anchovy paste

200 g (7 oz) cooked, skinless, boneless chicken breast

6 baby plum or cherry tomatoes

40 g (1½ oz) sea salt and black pepper or plain croûtons

4 teaspoons finely grated Parmesan cheese, to serve

freshly ground black pepper

1 Break the lettuce into separate leaves and tear these into pieces. Wash well in the colander; drain and share between 2 plates or bowls.

2 Cut the garlic clove in half, then rub the cut surfaces around the inside of a mixing bowl – you only want a hint of garlic. Add the soft cheese and beat it until smooth; then add the yogurt and anchovy paste, mixing until combined. Tear in the chicken and toss to coat it in the dressing.

3 Arrange the dressed chicken over the lettuce leaves. Halve the tomatoes and add them to the salad. Scatter an equal amount of croûtons over each portion and sprinkle 2 teaspoons of Parmesan cheese over each serving. Season with a little black pepper and serve.

Cook's tip If you choose not to use anchovy paste, you may need to season the dressing with a little salt.

Speedy chicken club

Pile a generous, tasty topping on slices of toast for lunch at home – or add another slice of bread and turn it into an easy-to-pack traditional sandwich for just 1 extra **ProPoints** value.

6 ProPoints value	
ProPoints values per serving	
ProPoints values per recipe	23
Serves 4	

At the ready

a toaster
a mixing bowl
kitchen scissors

Ingredients

4 slices Weight Watchers Malted Danish
    Loaf
40 g (1½ oz) low fat soft cheese
15 g (½ oz) reduced fat mayonnaise
15 g (½ oz) gherkins
2-3 crisp lettuce **leaves (Iceberg or**
    Romaine)
1 beef tomato
225 g (8 oz) skinless, boneless roast
    chicken slices
1 small ripe avocado
½ lemon or lime
salt and freshly ground black pepper
a small handful of fresh chives

1 Lightly toast the bread. While it is toasting, mix together the soft cheese and mayonnaise. Chop the gherkins and add them to the mixture. Spread over the slices of toast. Put the toast on 4 plates.

2 Shred the lettuce leaves and slice the beef tomato, and arrange them on the toast with the chicken. Peel and stone the avocado and slice it thinly; then share it between the portions and squeeze over the lemon or lime juice.

3 Season the open sandwiches; then snip the chives over them using scissors. Serve at once.

Cook's tip Slice the remaining lemon or lime into 4 and pop into glasses of water with lots of ice cubes.

To make a traditional sandwich Add another slice of bread per portion, but don't toast them, and spread the soft cheese mixture on both slices. This will add 1 extra **ProPoints** value per serving.

Quick chicken pasta

Filling pasta in a flash – an ideal midweek supper that all the family will enjoy.

ProPoints values per serving	
ProPoints values per recipe	**39**
Serves 4	

At the ready

a large saucepan
a kettle of boiling water
a garlic crusher
kitchen scissors
a colander

Ingredients

250 g (9 oz) tagliatelle
6 spring onions
1 large courgette
200 g (7 oz) green beans
200 g (7 oz) low fat soft cheese
125 ml (4 fl oz) skimmed milk
1 small garlic clove
a small handful of fresh flat leaf parsley
300 g (10½ oz) cooked, skinless, boneless chicken breast
freshly ground black pepper

1 Put the tagliatelle in the saucepan, cover with plenty of boiling water from the kettle and cook for 8 minutes.

2 Meanwhile, finely slice the spring onions; chop the courgette into small pieces; slice the green beans. Add these vegetables to the tagliatelle after it has cooked for 8 minutes. Cook for 2-3 more minutes, until the pasta is tender.

3 At the same time, stir the soft cheese and milk together, using a whisk or wooden spoon to give a smooth mixture. Crush the garlic clove directly into the mixture, then snip in about half the parsley using a pair of scissors. Season with black pepper and stir well. Slice the chicken thinly.

4 Reserve 2 tablespoons of the cooking liquid from the pasta, then drain the tagliatelle and vegetables in the colander. Return them to the saucepan with the reserved cooking liquid. Stir in the cheese mixture and sliced chicken. Heat gently for 1-2 minutes, stirring occasionally, until heated through.

5 Serve each portion on a warmed plate, snipping the rest of the parsley over the top, and season with a little extra black pepper.

Variation

Try using spaghetti or linguine instead of tagliatelle, or use pasta shapes such as penne, fusilli or farfalle.

Cook's tips Use asparagus when in season, instead of green beans.

If you roasted a chicken at the weekend, this is an ideal way to use up the leftovers for supper on Monday – for a *ProPoints* value of 11 per serving.

Fragrant Thai chicken

The beauty of Thai curries is that they are simple and quick to cook. So don't even think about ordering a take-away – try this home-made version instead. And once you've stocked up on the spices and sauces, you'll know you've always got the basics to hand any time you fancy a curry.

ProPoints values per serving	8 ProPoints value
ProPoints values per recipe	31
Serves 4	

At the ready

a wok or large deep frying pan
a measuring jug
a kettle of boiling water
kitchen scissors

Ingredients

450 g (1 lb) skinless, boneless chicken breast
calorie controlled cooking spray
400 g can reduced fat coconut milk
3 teaspoons chicken stock powder (or 1 chicken stock cube)
2 tablespoons Thai green curry paste
2 tablespoons fish sauce
1 stalk fresh lemongrass
a bunch of spring onions
1 large courgette
200 g (7 oz) fine asparagus
200 g (7 oz) mangetout **or** sugar snap peas
1 red chilli **(optional)**
a small handful of fresh coriander

1 Cut the chicken into chunks. Heat the wok or frying pan, spray with the cooking spray and stir-fry the chicken for 2 minutes.

2 Pour the coconut milk into the wok or frying pan and measure in 300 ml (10 fl oz) of boiling water from the kettle. Add the stock powder or crumble in the stock cube; then stir in the Thai curry paste and fish sauce. Bash the lemongrass with a rolling pin and add it to the wok or pan. Heat to a gentle simmer and cook for 5 minutes.

3 Meanwhile, thinly slice the spring onions and add them to the wok. Thinly slice the courgette and cut the asparagus spears into short lengths; add them to the wok with the mangetout or sugar snap peas. Remove the seeds from the red chilli (if using) and thinly slice it; then add it to the wok. Simmer for a further 10 minutes; then remove the lemongrass stalk.

4 Ladle the curry into warmed bowls and snip the coriander on top using a pair of scissors before serving.

Variation

Use Thai red curry paste instead of green, if you prefer.

Serving suggestion You can serve each portion with 75 g (3½ oz) cooked jasmine or basmati rice. This will add 3 *ProPoints* values per serving.

Cajun turkey salad

A gorgeous salad for two to share – great for lunch or a good option for when you're running out of **ProPoints** values at the end of the day.

ProPoints values per serving	
ProPoints values per recipe	**7**
Serves 2	

At the ready

a char-grill pan or grill
kitchen scissors

Ingredients

1 large courgette
calorie controlled cooking spray
2 x 125 g (4½ oz) turkey steaks
1 teaspoon Cajun seasoning
100 g (3½ oz) mixed salad leaves
2 roasted red peppers (from a jar, packed
   in brine), torn into pieces
2 plum tomatoes, **quartered**
1 lime or ½ lemon
freshly ground black pepper

1 Heat the char-grill pan or grill. Meanwhile, slice the courgette at a steep angle to give long, thin slices. Spray them with the cooking spray and cook in batches in the char-grill pan or under the grill, until tender. Set aside.

2 Spray the turkey steaks with the cooking spray, sprinkle both sides with the Cajun seasoning and char-grill or grill for 3-4 minutes on each side.

3 While the turkey is cooking, arrange the salad leaves on a serving platter with the red peppers, tomatoes and char-grilled courgettes.

4 When the turkey steaks are cooked, transfer them to a chopping board and let them rest for 2 minutes. Then slice them into thin strips and arrange on top of the salad. Squeeze the lime or lemon juice over, season with ground black pepper, then serve.

Variation

You could use **skinless, boneless chicken breasts** instead of turkey steaks for the same **ProPoints** values. Before cooking, cover them with cling film and beat them with a rolling pin until flattened.

Cook's tip **Use any leaves you like, such as Romaine or Iceberg** lettuce, watercress, spinach, rocket **or** chard **– they will all work well in this salad.**

Summer vegetable and turkey linguine

Turkey rashers are so versatile and satisfying – keep a pack in the fridge for dishes such as this tasty pasta supper.

ProPoints values per serving	10
ProPoints values per recipe	38
Serves 4	

At the ready

- **a large saucepan**
- **a kettle of boiling water**
- **a non-stick frying pan**
- **kitchen scissors**
- **a food processor with slicer attachment**
- **a colander**

Ingredients

- **250 g (9 oz) linguine or spaghetti**
- **calorie controlled cooking spray**
- **200 g pack lightly smoked turkey rashers**
- **4 spring onions**
- **1 large courgette**
- **100 g (3½ oz) frozen petits pois or garden peas**
- **200 g (7 oz) low fat soft cheese**
- **125 ml (4 fl oz) skimmed milk**
- **a small handful of fresh chives**
- **freshly ground black pepper**

1 Put the linguine or spaghetti into the saucepan and cover with plenty of boiling water from the kettle. Cook for 8 minutes, or according to the packet instructions.

2 At the same time, heat the frying pan and spray it with the cooking spray. Snip in the turkey rashers with a pair of scissors and cook them for 2-3 minutes. Remove the pan from the heat and set aside.

3 Finely slice the spring onions. Slice the courgette thinly, either in the food processor or by hand. Add the spring onions, courgette and peas to the spaghetti or linguine after it has cooked for 8 minutes. Cook for 2 more minutes.

4 Meanwhile, stir the soft cheese and milk together, using a whisk or wooden spoon to give a smooth mixture. Snip the chives into the mixture with scissors and season with black pepper.

5 Reserve 2 tablespoons of the cooking liquid from the pasta; then drain the pasta through the colander. Return the pasta to the saucepan with the reserved cooking liquid. Stir in the cheese mixture; then add the turkey rashers. Heat gently for 1-2 minutes, stirring occasionally. Serve in warmed bowls or on plates.

Serving suggestion

Serve with a teaspoon of finely grated Parmesan cheese per serving for an extra 1 **ProPoints** value per person.

Cook's tip Use any shape of pasta that you happen to have in your cupboard.

Awaken your tastebuds A hint of fresh chilli, added to the frying pan with the turkey rashers, is great if you like your pasta hotter. Just de-seed and thinly slice 1 chilli, and use according to taste.

Superfast turkey meatballs

An old family favourite for a weekday supper, served with a substantial vegetable sauce. And, yes, you can get it on the table in 20 minutes.

ProPoints values per serving	10 ProPoints value
ProPoints values per recipe	39
Serves 4	

At the ready

- **a large non-stick frying pan**
- **a measuring jug**
- **a kettle of boiling water**
- **a food processor with standard blade**
- **a mixing bowl**
- **a large saucepan**
- **a colander**

Ingredients

- **2 x 400 g cans chopped** tomatoes
- **2 teaspoons dried mixed Italian herbs**
- **2 teaspoons chicken or vegetable stock powder (or 1 cube)**
- **1 large** onion
- **1 large** garlic clove
- **1** courgette
- **1** carrot
- **400 g (14 oz) turkey mince**
- **1 teaspoon dried thyme**
- **250 g (9 oz) dried pasta shapes**
- **salt and freshly ground black pepper**
- fresh basil **leaves, to garnish**

excluding pasta

1. Tip the cans of tomatoes into the large frying pan and add the dried Italian herbs. Measure in 150 ml (5 fl oz) boiling water from the kettle and add the stock powder or crumble in the cube. Turn on the heat.

2. While the tomatoes are heating, chop the onion and garlic finely in the food processor. Spoon half the chopped onion and garlic mixture into the mixing bowl, and the rest into the tomatoes.

3. Chop the courgette and carrot finely in the food processor. Add them into the pan of tomatoes and stir well. Bring the heat to a brisk simmer.

4. Put the turkey mince and thyme into the mixing bowl with the remaining onion and garlic. Season and mix thoroughly. Form the mixture into small meatballs (it helps if you have wet hands), adding them to the tomato sauce as you make them. Keep the sauce simmering briskly, and cook for 12 minutes, turning the meatballs occasionally. Add a little extra water if needed.

5. At the same time, put the pasta in the saucepan and cover with plenty of boiling water from the kettle. Cook for 8-10 minutes, or according to the packet instructions.

6. Drain the pasta in the colander and share between 4 warmed plates or bowls. Serve with the meatballs and tomato sauce, scattered with basil leaves, to garnish.

Variation

You could use **extra-lean minced beef** instead of turkey. The **ProPoints** values per serving would be 9.

> **Not pushed for time?** Cook the meatballs for longer, cover the pan, turn the heat to very low and simmer gently for 35-40 minutes – the flavours will be intensified by the slower cooking time. Cook the dried pasta for the final 8-10 minutes.

"My life is made easier by weighing out little bags of rice and pasta. I do this when I buy a big bag so I've always got it handy for a quick meal. I do the same with cereals, which saves time during the morning rush."

Lana McLaughlin Weight Watchers member

Fish + Seafood

Keralan fish curry

For a Friday night curry, you can't beat this mild, fragrant south Indian-style fish recipe that makes the most of inexpensive frozen pollock.

ProPoints values per serving

ProPoints values per recipe	**40**
Serves 4	

At the ready

a wok or large deep frying pan

a garlic crusher

a measuring jug

a kettle of boiling water

a saucepan

Ingredients

300 ml (10½ fl oz) reduced fat coconut milk

2 tablespoons korma curry paste

2 teaspoons finely chopped fresh or 'lazy' ginger

1 large garlic clove

2 teaspoons vegetable stock powder (or 1 stock cube)

400g can cherry tomatoes or chopped tomatoes

1 teaspoon dried curry leaves

175 g (6 oz) basmati rice

450 g (1 lb) frozen pollock steaks

100 g (3½ oz) sugar snap peas or mangetout

100 g (3½ oz) broccoli, broken into florets

1 lime, quartered, to serve (optional)

salt and freshly ground black pepper

1 Pour the coconut milk into the wok or frying pan and turn on the heat. Add the curry paste and chopped ginger. Crush the garlic directly into the wok, using the garlic crusher (or chop it finely).

2 Measure 300 ml (10 fl oz) of boiling water from the kettle into the wok or frying pan; stir in the stock powder, or crumble in the stock cube. Add the can of tomatoes and the curry leaves. Simmer briskly for 5 minutes.

3 Meanwhile, put the rice in the saucepan and cover with plenty of boiling water from the kettle. Cook for 12 minutes, or until tender.

4 Cut the frozen fish into large chunks. Add them to the wok or frying pan with the sugar snap peas or mangetout and broccoli when the coconut milk mixture has been simmering for 5 minutes. Check the seasoning. Turn the heat to low and continue to cook gently for 6-7 minutes.

5 Drain the rice and share between 4 warmed bowls or plates. Spoon the fish curry on the side. Serve with the lime quarters, if using.

Variation

You could make the curry with 450 g (1 lb) **frozen mixed seafood** instead. Just add it to the curry sauce as above, from frozen, and let it simmer in the sauce for a couple of extra minutes – 8-9 minutes altogether. This will work out at 11 **ProPoints** values per serving.

Cook's tip Why not make a cooling raita to accompany the curry? Simply chop ¼ cucumber finely and mix it with 150 g (5½ fl oz) low fat plain yogurt and a few fresh mint leaves, snipped into tiny pieces. This will add 1 *ProPoints* value per serving.

Smoked haddock Florentine

This is a great fish dish for one – though it's easy enough to scale it up for more people if you need to.

ProPoints values per serving	**5** ProPoints value
ProPoints values per recipe	5
Serves 1	

At the ready

a frying pan
a kettle of boiling water
a small saucepan
a colander

Ingredients

175 g (6 oz) skinless smoked haddock
fillet
a few drops of vinegar
1 egg
150 g (5½ oz) young leaf spinach
freshly ground black pepper

1 Put the smoked haddock fillet into the frying pan and pour in boiling water from the kettle to just cover it. Put the pan on the heat and simmer gently for 5-6 minutes, until the flesh is opaque and flakes easily when tested with a fork.

2 When the fish has been cooking for about 3 minutes, half-fill the saucepan with boiling water and add a few drops of vinegar. Re-fill the kettle and put it on to boil. Crack the egg into the saucepan and poach it gently for 3-4 minutes, depending on how you like it cooked.

3 Meanwhile, pack the spinach into the colander. It will look like a huge amount, but it soon reduces down. Slowly pour boiling water from the kettle over the spinach, to wilt the leaves. Press the leaves down with the back of a wooden spoon to squeeze out more moisture.

4 Put the spinach on a warmed plate. Lift the haddock out of the frying pan using a draining spoon and lay it on top of the spinach. Lift the poached egg from the saucepan using the same spoon, and sit it on top of the fish. Season with black pepper and serve at once.

Variation

Look out for **smoked pollock** or **smoked cod fillets**, which could be used instead of the haddock. You could also use frozen fish – it will only take another couple of minutes to cook.

As an alternative **Serve the fish and poached egg on top of a mound of mashed** potatoes, **with chopped** fresh parsley **stirred into it. If you use 225 g (8 oz) mash instead of spinach, it will work out at 10** *ProPoints* **values per serving.**

Salmon kachumber

A date-night supper for two with grilled salmon, basmati rice and a refreshing Indian-style salad.

ProPoints values per serving	**10**
ProPoints values per recipe	21
Serves 2	

At the ready

- **a saucepan**
- **a kettle of boiling water**
- **a fine grater**

Ingredients

- **100 g (3½ oz) basmati rice**
- **2 x 120 g (4¼ oz) salmon fillets**
- **1 small lemon**
- **1 teaspoon cumin seeds**
- **1 red onion**
- **1 green chilli**
- **2 tomatoes**
- **¼ cucumber**
- **a small handful of fresh mint**
- **a small handful of fresh coriander**
- **salt and freshly ground black pepper**

1 Put the rice in the saucepan and cover with plenty of boiling water from the kettle. Cook for 12 minutes, or according to the packet instructions.

2 At the same time, preheat the grill. Cover the grill pan with a piece of foil. Arrange the salmon fillets on the grill rack and grate the zest from the lemon over them. Squeeze the juice from half the lemon over the fillets; then sprinkle them with the cumin seeds. Grill for 6-8 minutes, until the flesh is opaque and flakes easily when tested with a fork.

3 Meanwhile, make the salad by finely chopping the onion, chilli (removing the seeds), tomatoes, cucumber, mint and coriander (reserving a few sprigs, for garnish). You could chop the ingredients in the food processor if you prefer, though it only takes a few minutes by hand. Season and add a squeeze of lemon juice.

4 Drain the rice and share it between 2 plates. Serve with the salmon and spoon the salad alongside, garnished with the reserved coriander and mint.

Variation

This dish works just as well with other types of fish: try it with **haddock**, **cod**, **coley** or **whiting** for a change.

Cook's tip If you have some spare *ProPoints* values serve each portion with a warm 44 g Weight Watchers mini plain naan bread – just add 3 *ProPoints* values per serving.

My Thai fish

Once you've got the ingredients in your storecupboard, you'll want to make this fish curry again and again. You can have it on the table in pretty much the same time as you'd spend queueing up for a take-away.

ProPoints values per serving	**5** ProPoints value
ProPoints values per recipe	**22**
Serves 4	

At the ready

a measuring jug

a kettle of boiling water

a wok or large saucepan

Ingredients

4 x 15 g sachets of instant miso soup paste

2 teaspoons prepared ginger paste

2 teaspoons prepared lemongrass paste

1 red or green chilli (optional)

2 x 50 g (1¾ oz) nests of fine egg noodles

350 g pack fresh stir-fry vegetables with beansprouts

2 heads pak choi

4 x 125 g (4½ oz) haddock, pollock or coley fillets

finely grated zest of 1 lime

a few sprigs of fresh coriander, to serve

1 Measure 1.2 litres (2 pints) of boiling water from the kettle into the wok or saucepan. Add the miso soup paste (see Cook's tip) and stir to dissolve. Add the ginger paste and lemongrass paste, and stir again while bringing the liquid back to the boil over a medium heat.

2 Thinly slice the chilli (if using), removing the seeds. Add it to the wok or saucepan with the noodles and cook for 3 minutes; then add the bag of stir-fry vegetables. Break up the pak choi into separate leaves and add these too.

3 As soon as you have added the pak choi, arrange the fish fillets on top and cover the wok with a lid or a piece of foil. Cook gently over a low heat to steam the fish for 5-6 minutes.

4 Ladle into warmed bowls and serve scattered with lime zest and coriander sprigs.

Variations

You could use different fish, such as **monkfish** or **whiting**.

Add some large cooked, peeled **prawns** just before serving. By adding 175 g (6 oz) you will increase the **ProPoints** values to 6 per serving.

Cook's tip If you can't find miso soup paste, use 4 rounded teaspoons of vegetable stock powder, or 1½ vegetable stock cubes.

Seared tuna Niçoise

Treat your partner – or a friend or fellow member – to a sophisticated fish supper when you've got 10 **ProPoints** values in hand.

ProPoints values per serving	**10** ProPoints value
ProPoints values per recipe	**20**
Serves 2	

At the ready

a saucepan

a kettle of boiling water

a char-grill pan or frying pan

a mixing bowl

kitchen scissors

a colander

Ingredients

250 g (9 oz) baby new potatoes

200 g (7 oz) fine green beans

2 tomatoes

2 tablespoons capers

10 black or green olives

2 teaspoons olive oil

2 teaspoons wholegrain mustard

1 lemon

a few sprigs of fresh flat leaf parsley

calorie controlled cooking spray

2 x 150 g (5½ oz) fresh tuna steaks

freshly ground black pepper

1 Halve the new potatoes; then put them in the saucepan, cover them with plenty of boiling water from the kettle and cook for 12 minutes. Slice the green beans in half, into the saucepan, and cook for 3 more minutes. Now preheat the char-grill pan or frying pan.

2 Meanwhile, quarter or chop the tomatoes and put them in the mixing bowl with the capers, olives, olive oil, mustard and juice of ½ the lemon. Snip in the parsley, using a pair of scissors.

3 Spray the cooking spray on both sides of the tuna steaks; add them to the hot char-grill pan or frying pan and cook for 2-3 minutes per side, depending on their thickness and how well done you like them.

4 Drain the potatoes and beans in the colander. Tip them into the bowl with the tomatoes and stir everything together. Share the salad between 2 warmed plates. Serve with the tuna steaks and season with black pepper. Serve with the remaining lemon, cut into wedges.

Variation

Try using different types of meaty fish – such as marlin or **swordfish**.

Cook's tip When using a char-grill pan, always spray the food, not the pan, with calorie controlled cooking spray.

Topsy-turvy fish pie

All the flavours of fish pie, but without the long wait – perfect for a fast family supper.

ProPoints values per serving	**10** ProPoints value
ProPoints values per recipe	**40**
Serves 4	

At the ready

- **a large saucepan**
- **a kettle of boiling water**
- **a small saucepan**
- **a large non-stick saucepan**
- **kitchen scissors**
- **a potato masher**

Ingredients

- **700 g (1 lb 9 oz) potatoes**
- **2 eggs**
- **450 ml (16 fl oz) skimmed milk**
- **40 g (1½ oz) plain flour**
- **1 tablespoon low fat spread**
- **2 tablespoons chopped fresh parsley or chives**
- **300 g (10½ oz) fish pie mix**
- **salt and freshly ground black pepper**

1 Peel and cut the potatoes into small chunks. Put them into the large saucepan and cover with plenty of boiling water from the kettle, then cover and simmer briskly for 12-15 minutes, until tender.

2 At the same time, put the eggs on to boil in the small saucepan for 10 minutes.

3 Meanwhile make the sauce. Reserve 2 tablespoons of milk and put the rest into the large non-stick saucepan with the flour and low fat spread. Bring up to the boil, stirring constantly with a small whisk, until the sauce thickens and boils. Reduce the heat. Snip in most of the parsley or chives with a pair of scissors and season. Tip in the chunks of fish and cook gently for 4-5 minutes, stirring occasionally – do this gently to avoid breaking up the fish.

4 Drain the eggs, shell them and cut them into quarters. Drain and mash the potatoes, beating in the reserved 2 tablespoons of milk. Season with some ground black pepper. Reheat for a few seconds, beating with a wooden spoon.

5 Share the mashed potato between 4 warmed plates. Spoon the fish mixture on top and arrange the eggs around the sides. Snip a little more parsley or chives on top and season with a little extra black pepper. Serve at once with a green vegetable such as broccoli.

Cook's tips

You can buy silicone-coated whisks that won't scratch the surface of non-stick pans – ideal for making all-in-one sauces like this.

Fish pie mix is generally made up of equal quantities of haddock, smoked haddock and salmon. You could buy separate pieces of fish to make up the same combination.

Far-flung prawns

Liven up a midweek supper with spicy prawns and noodles. If you've got prawns in the freezer and a well-stocked storecupboard, you need never be stuck for inspiration or tempted to pick up a take-away on the way home.

ProPoints values per serving	
ProPoints values per recipe	20
Serves 2	

At the ready

a small mixing bowl

a fine grater

a large heatproof bowl

a kettle of boiling water

a colander

a non-stick frying pan

Ingredients

250 g (9 oz) large cooked, peeled prawns, thawed if frozen

2 tablespoons sweet chilli sauce

1 lime

¼ cucumber

300 g pack ready-cooked fine rice noodles

1 Little Gem lettuce

2 teaspoons toasted sesame oil

2 teaspoons soy sauce

freshly ground black pepper

a small handful of fresh mint leaves

2 teaspoons sesame seeds

1 Put the prawns in the small mixing bowl and add the sweet chilli sauce. Grate in the zest from the lime; then squeeze in the juice from ½ the lime. Chop the cucumber finely and add to the bowl; toss to coat the prawns and cucumber in the dressing.

2 Put the noodles into the heatproof bowl and pour over enough boiling water from the kettle to cover them. Leave for 2 minutes.

3 Meanwhile, break the lettuce into separate leaves, wash well and drain in the colander; then arrange the leaves on 2 plates.

4 Drain the noodles thoroughly in the colander. Return them to the bowl they were in and add the sesame oil, soy sauce and remaining lime juice, tossing them gently to coat them in the dressing. Pile the noodles on the lettuce leaves.

5 Spoon the prawn mixture on to the noodles. Season with a little black pepper and scatter the mint leaves on top. Finally, toast the sesame seeds in the dry frying pan for 1-2 minutes and sprinkle them over the salads. Serve immediately.

Variation

Use **fresh coriander** instead of fresh mint, for a change.

Cook's tip You could use small North Atlantic prawns instead of large ones – they have a great flavour, and they don't take long to thaw if you keep a pack in the freezer.

Fish lovers' sweet and sour

Another home-made take-away style meal without any of the drawbacks of ordering out. Start with a bowl of Easy Chinese Soup (see page 20) and you'll still stay within 10 **ProPoints** values for dinner.

ProPoints values per serving	
ProPoints values per recipe	**40**
Serves 4	

At the ready

- **a food processor with slicing attachment**
- **a wok or large frying pan**
- **a measuring jug**
- **a kettle of boiling water**
- **a saucepan**
- **a small mixing bowl**

Ingredients

1 large carrot

1 onion

3 teaspoons vegetable stock powder (or 1 cube)

2 tablespoons tomato purée

180 g (6 oz) long grain rice

100 g (3½ oz) mangetout or sugar snap peas

300 g (10½ oz) skinless salmon fillet

3 tomatoes

227 g can pineapple chunks in juice

200 g (7 oz) large cooked, peeled prawns

1 tablespoon cornflour

1 tablespoon vinegar

2 tablespoons soy sauce

salt and freshly ground black pepper

1 Slice the carrot and onion in the food processor. Put them into the wok or large frying pan and add 400 ml (14 fl oz) boiling water from the kettle. Add the stock powder or crumble in the stock cube, stir in the tomato purée and bring to a brisk simmer. Cook for 5 minutes.

2 Meanwhile, put the rice into the saucepan and cover with plenty of boiling water from the kettle. Cook for 12 minutes, until tender.

3 When the carrot and onion have cooked for 5 minutes, add the mangetout or sugar snap peas. Cut the salmon into chunks and add to the vegetables. Chop the tomatoes roughly and add them too. Reduce the heat and simmer for 2-3 minutes.

4 Drain the pineapple juice into the small mixing bowl and tip the pineapple chunks in with the salmon. Add the prawns and continue to cook over a low heat for 2 minutes.

5 Blend the cornflour, vinegar and soy sauce into the pineapple juice; then tip the mixture into the wok or frying pan, stirring gently for about 1 minute, until smooth and thickened. Check the seasoning. Drain the rice, share between 4 warmed plates and serve with the sweet and sour seafood.

> **Cook's tip** You could use fresh pineapple, if you like. You would need to blend the cornflour with 2 tablespoons of cold water, instead of using the pineapple juice from the can. This will have a *ProPoints* value of 9 per serving.

"Cauliflower – puréed with roasted garlic instead of mash, stir-fried with spring onions and a little sesame oil instead of rice, or blitzed in a blender instead of couscous – just a delicious low carb swap."

Nicola Strawbridge Weight Watchers member

Vegetarian

Giant couscous salad

A portion of this tasty salad makes an ideal lunch – at home or packed up to take to work.

ProPoints values per serving	
ProPoints values per recipe	32
Serves 4	

At the ready

a kettle of boiling water

a large saucepan on the hob

a fine grater

a non-stick frying pan

a food processor with slicing attachment

Ingredients

1 large red pepper

1 large yellow pepper

3 teaspoons vegetable stock powder
(or 1 vegetable stock cube)

200 g (7 oz) giant couscous

1 lemon

200 g (7 oz) reduced fat halloumi cheese

1 red onion

85 g bag fresh rocket

a handful of fresh mint **leaves**

freshly ground black pepper

1 Preheat the grill. Slice each pepper into 4-5 pieces, discarding the core and seeds; then arrange them on the grill rack, skin side up. Grill for 15 minutes, turning once.

2 Meanwhile, pour the boiling water from the kettle into the saucepan until it's half-full. Stir in the vegetable stock powder or crumble in the stock cube. Add the couscous and grate the zest from the lemon directly into the saucepan. Give everything a stir and bring back to the boil; reduce the heat and simmer gently for 10-12 minutes until the couscous is soft and translucent.

3 While the couscous is cooking, slice the halloumi and dry-fry in a non-stick frying pan for 4-5 minutes until browned, turning once.

4 Thinly slice the red onion in the food processor and tip it into a salad bowl. Halve the lemon and squeeze in the juice.

5 Drain the couscous, rinse it with cold water and drain again thoroughly. Add it to the salad bowl. Tear the grilled peppers into pieces and add them to the bowl. Add the bag of rocket and toss everything together. Season with black pepper and serve scattered with the halloumi cheese slices, broken up, and mint leaves.

Cook's tip **If you haven't tried giant couscous before, it has a deliciously different texture to regular couscous – though, of course, you can use that instead. (Regular couscous will need only 5 minutes to cook.)**

Taking the salad to work? **Pack the rocket leaves and mint separately and stir them through just before serving, to prevent them from wilting.**

Veggie filo tart

After a busy day, put this lovely summery tart together in no time and before you know it, you'll be eating supper in the garden. It's perfect for weekends, too – take it to the park or beach as part of a picnic.

ProPoints values per serving	
ProPoints values per recipe	**20**
Serves 4	

At the ready

a Swiss roll tin or large baking sheet

a large saucepan on the hob

a kettle of boiling water

a food processor with slicer attachment

Ingredients

calorie controlled cooking spray

4 x 45 g (1½ oz) sheets of Jus-Rol filo pastry, measuring 50 x 24 cm (20 x 9½ inches), thawed if frozen

150 g (5½ oz) fine asparagus

1 large courgette

4 spring onions

8 cherry tomatoes

1 large egg

100 g (3½ oz) reduced fat crème fraîche

1 teaspoon dried oregano or mixed Italian herbs

salt and freshly ground black pepper

fresh basil or rocket leaves, to serve

1 Preheat the oven to Gas Mark 7/220°C/fan oven 200°C. Spray the Swiss roll tin or large baking sheet with the cooking spray.

2 Lay 2 sheets of filo pastry on the tin or baking sheet (they will overhang it at the moment) and spray them with the cooking spray. Lay the other 2 sheets on top and spray once more. Scrunch up the edges to fit the tin, to form a border. Bake the pastry in the oven for 3-4 minutes.

3 Put the asparagus into the saucepan and cover with boiling water from the kettle. Boil for 2 minutes.

4 While the asparagus is cooking, slice the courgette and spring onions in the food processor. Halve the cherry tomatoes. Drain the asparagus. Beat the egg, crème fraîche and herbs together and season.

5 Take the filo tart out of the oven and pour the egg mixture on top of it. Scatter the courgette, spring onions, asparagus and cherry tomatoes over the surface. Bake for a further 10-12 minutes until the egg mixture is set.

6 Cool the tart for a few minutes; cut it into quarters and serve warm or cold, scattered with the basil or rocket leaves.

Variation

Replace the asparagus with strips of roasted red pepper (from a jar, packed in brine).

> Cook's tip **Return any unused filo pastry to the packet, wrap in cling film and refrigerate; you can keep it for 3-4 days to use in another recipe.**

Quorn tikka salad

This lively salad has an Indian influence. Serve it with a warm 44 g Weight Watchers mini plain naan bread – just add 3 **ProPoints** values per serving. Try packing up a portion to take to work.

ProPoints values per serving	
ProPoints values per recipe	**8**
Serves 2	

At the ready

a shallow bowl

a small bowl

Ingredients

5 tablespoons low fat plain yogurt

1 teaspoon tikka curry powder

140 g pack Quorn roast-style sliced fillets

a small handful of fresh mint **or**
    coriander **leaves**

75 g (2¾ oz) mixed salad leaves

8 radishes

1 small red onion

¼ cucumber

8 cherry tomatoes

1 Put 2 tablespoons of the yogurt into a shallow bowl and stir in the tikka powder. Add the Quorn roast-style sliced fillets and stir to coat.

2 Put the remaining yogurt in a small bowl. Chop some of the mint or coriander finely and stir into the yogurt. Set aside.

3 Share the salad leaves between 2 serving plates. Thinly slice the radishes, red onion and cucumber and arrange an equal amount over each salad. Halve the cherry tomatoes and divide between the salads.

4 Spoon the Quorn fillets on top of the salads and drizzle them with the yogurt dressing.

Cook's tip To save time, you could slice the radishes, red onion and cucumber in your food processor, fitted with the slicer attachment.

Stuffed mega-mushrooms

Try these Mediterranean style mushrooms for a light lunch or supper – or serve them as a dinner-party starter with a salad garnish.

ProPoints values per serving	6 ProPoints value
ProPoints values per recipe	25
Serves 4	

At the ready

a roasting tin

a kettle of boiling water

a large measuring jug

a large heatproof bowl

a fine grater

a non-stick frying pan

Ingredients

calorie controlled cooking spray

4 very large mushrooms, such as portobello

2 teaspoons vegetable stock powder (or vegetable stock cube)

1 lemon

200 g (7 oz) couscous

a bunch of spring onions

2 roasted red peppers (from a jar, packed in brine)

1 large tomato

100 g (3½ oz) reduced fat feta cheese

1 teaspoon fresh thyme leaves, plus a few sprigs (optional)

freshly ground black pepper

1. Preheat the oven to Gas Mark 6/200°C/fan oven 180°C. Spray the roasting tin with the cooking spray. Remove and reserve the stalks from the mushrooms and put the caps in the roasting tin, brown gills facing upwards. Spray with the cooking spray and roast in the oven for 5-6 minutes.

2. Meanwhile, measure 250 ml (9 fl oz) boiling water from the kettle and pour into the heatproof bowl. Add the stock powder or crumble in the stock cube. Finely grate the zest from the lemon directly into the bowl and stir well. Add the couscous and stir again; cover and set aside for 5 minutes, until the liquid has been absorbed.

3. While the couscous is soaking, finely chop the spring onions and mushroom stalks. Heat the non-stick frying pan, spray with the cooking spray and cook the spring onions and mushroom stalks gently for 3 minutes.

4. Tip the spring onion mixture into the soaked couscous and add a squeeze of lemon juice. Tear the roasted red peppers into pieces and add them to the bowl. Chop the tomato and add it to the bowl. Crumble in the feta cheese and add the thyme leaves, if using.

5. Take the mushrooms out of the oven and spoon in the couscous filling. Garnish with a few thyme sprigs, if using, and season with black pepper. Cover with a piece of foil and roast for a further 12 minutes.

Variation

If you have a little more time, use the stuffing to fill halved red or yellow **peppers** – they will take about 20-25 minutes to cook.

Cook's tip If you can't find the very large mushrooms, just use 2 smaller ones per portion.

For a more hearty main meal Make this recipe for two people rather than four, for 12 *ProPoints* values per serving.

Tortilla pizzas

Enjoy a pizza for just 5 **ProPoints** values. The kids will enjoy them, too, so there's no need to cook them something separately.

ProPoints values per serving	
ProPoints values per recipe	**21**
Serves 4	

At the ready

2 large baking sheets

Ingredients

calorie controlled cooking spray

4 Weight Watchers soft flour tortillas

150 g jar tomato pizza topping

100 g (3½ oz) reduced fat grated Cheddar cheese

4 tomatoes, thinly sliced

2 teaspoons dried mixed Italian herbs

freshly ground black pepper

12 black olives, halved (optional)

fresh basil leaves, to garnish (optional)

1 Preheat the oven to Gas Mark 6/200°C/fan oven 180°C. Spray the baking sheets with the cooking spray.

2 Put two tortillas on each baking sheet, then spread the jar of pizza topping equally over each one. Arrange the cheese and sliced tomatoes on top and sprinkle with dried herbs. Season with a little black pepper. Scatter the olives on top, if using.

3 Bake for 8-10 minutes. Slide the pizzas on to plates and serve, scattered with basil leaves, if using.

Variation

Vary the topping: try torn roasted red peppers (from a jar, packed in brine) or **courgette** slices. When they're in season, add a few fine **asparagus** spears, cut into short lengths and boiled for 3-4 minutes before adding to the topping.

Cook's tip If your baking sheets aren't big enough for 2 tortillas, cook the pizzas in two batches.

Freeze any unused tortillas Just make sure that they are well wrapped to exclude air. Freeze them for up to 3 months. Or use them in the speedy Veggie Chilli recipe on page 108.

Veggie chilli with baked tortilla chips and carrot salsa

Try this super-quick vegetarian chilli, served with clever tortilla chips made from Weight Watchers soft flour tortillas, cut into triangles and baked. It makes a great midweek supper.

ProPoints values per serving	
ProPoints values per recipe	28
Serves 4	

At the ready

2 baking sheets
a large saucepan on the hob
a grater
kitchen scissors

Ingredients

calorie controlled cooking spray
300 g pack frozen Quorn mince
420 g can mixed beans in chilli sauce
300 g jar mild salsa
400 g can cherry tomatoes
1-2 teaspoons mild chilli powder
200 g (7 oz) mushrooms
4 Weight Watchers soft flour tortillas

For the carrot salsa

1 carrot
¼ cucumber
a small handful of fresh coriander or mint
1-2 teaspoons vinegar or lime juice
salt and freshly ground black pepper

  excluding salad

1. Preheat the oven to Gas Mark 6/200°C/fan oven 180°C. Spray the baking sheets with the cooking spray.

2. Tip the frozen Quorn mince into the saucepan and add the mixed beans in chilli sauce, jar of salsa, canned cherry tomatoes and chilli powder. Stir well and bring to the boil.

3. Meanwhile, thinly slice the mushrooms. Add them to the saucepan and stir; then turn down the heat so that the sauce is simmering. Cook for 15 minutes.

4. While the chilli is cooking, prepare the carrot salsa. Coarsely grate the carrot (do this in your food processor if you prefer). Finely chop the cucumber and coriander or mint and mix everything together with 1-2 teaspoons of vinegar or lime juice. Season with a little salt and pepper.

5. Five minutes before the chilli is ready, cut each tortilla into 8 triangles using a pair of scissors. Arrange them on the baking sheets and bake for 3-4 minutes, until crisp.

6. Serve the chilli on warmed plates or in bowls, with the salsa and baked tortilla chips.

Cook's tip Bulk out the chilli a bit more by adding a grated carrot and a grated courgette. The good news is you won't be adding any *ProPoints* values.

Feeling hungry? If you have some *ProPoints* values to spare, serve each portion with 75 g (2¾ oz) cooked long grain rice. This will add 3 *ProPoints* values per serving.

Tex-Mex omelette burritos

A brilliant solution for breakfast on the run: an omelette-filled tortilla that you can take with you to eat later. It's a great idea for a packed lunch or light meal, too.

ProPoints values per serving | **6** ProPoints value

ProPoints values per recipe   13
Serves 2

At the ready

a food processor with standard blade
a non-stick frying pan

Ingredients

2 tomatoes
¼ cucumber
1 small red onion
a small handful of fresh coriander **or**
     parsley
2 Weight Watchers soft flour tortillas
3 eggs
3 tablespoons skimmed milk
calorie controlled cooking spray
25 g (1 oz) reduced fat cheese, grated
salt and freshly ground black pepper

1   Finely chop the tomatoes, cucumber, red onion and coriander or parsley in the food processor, or chop finely with a cook's knife if you prefer. Take care not to over-process the vegetables, or they will become too wet.

2   Lay out the tortillas on a work surface. Preheat the grill. Beat the eggs and milk together and season lightly.

3   Heat a non-stick frying pan and spray with the cooking spray. Pour in half the beaten egg mixture. Cook on the hob over a medium heat for a few moments to set the base. Sprinkle half the tomato mixture over the surface and sprinkle half the cheese over the top. Grill the surface to set the egg and melt the cheese.

4   Slide the omelette on to one of the tortillas. Season it and leave it to cool a little while you make the second omelette. Place it on top of the second tortilla.

5   Roll up the tortillas and slice them in half. Serve immediately, or wrap in foil to serve later.

Cook's tip **If you're not keen on raw onion, simply leave it out, or replace it with a small red, green or yellow** pepper**, finely chopped.**

For a touch of spicy heat **Sprinkle a little finely chopped red or green** chilli **over the omelette before adding the cheese, or use a pinch of dried chilli.**

Easy peasy pasta

Low fat soft cheese makes a super-creamy sauce for pasta in this simple recipe with peas, broccoli, lemon zest and chopped fresh herbs.

ProPoints values per serving	
ProPoints values per recipe	**38**
Serves 4	

At the ready

- **a large saucepan on the hob**
- **a kettle of boiling water**
- **a colander**
- **kitchen scissors**

Ingredients

- **250 g (9 oz) dried pasta shapes, such as penne or fusilli**
- **a bunch of** spring onions
- **400 g (14 oz)** broccoli
- **200 g (7 oz) frozen** petits pois **or** garden peas
- **200 g tub low fat soft cheese**
- **150 ml (5 fl oz)** skimmed milk
- **1 lemon**
- **a small handful of** fresh flat leaf parsley **or** chives
- **salt and freshly ground black pepper**
- **4 teaspoons finely grated vegetarian Parmesan cheese, to serve (optional)**

1. Put the pasta shapes in the saucepan and cover with plenty of boiling water from the kettle. Cook for 8 minutes, or according to the packet instructions.

2. Meanwhile, slice the spring onions and break the broccoli into small florets. Add them to the pasta and cook for a further 2-3 minutes.

3. Put the frozen peas in the colander. When the pasta and broccoli are ready, drain them in the colander over the peas, reserving 2 tablespoons of the cooking water.

4. Put the soft cheese and skimmed milk into the hot saucepan with the reserved cooking water and stir with a whisk or wooden spoon over a medium-high heat to make a smooth sauce. Grate the zest from the lemon directly into the saucepan; then, using kitchen scissors, snip in the parsley or chives.

5. Return the pasta, broccoli and peas to the saucepan and stir gently over a low heat for 1-2 minutes.

6. Season, then serve, sprinkling each portion with 1 teaspoon of grated cheese, if using, and garnishing with extra black pepper.

Variation

You could add a chopped **courgette** to the recipe, too – just add it to the pasta with the broccoli – without adding **ProPoints** values.

> **Cook's tips** Use any pasta shapes you like – including spaghetti or linguine.
>
> If using the Parmesan cheese, check the packet, or ask the retailer, to make sure the cheese is suitable for vegetarians.

Mediterranean chilli tomato tagliatelle

Chilli, cherry tomatoes and char-grilled asparagus combine in this summery pasta dish. It's simple, quick and really tasty.

ProPoints values per serving	7 ProPoints value
ProPoints values per recipe	**27**
Serves 4	

At the ready

a char-grill pan (or use the grill)

a large saucepan on the hob

a kettle of boiling water

a colander

kitchen scissors

Ingredients

450 g (1 lb) fine asparagus spears

calorie controlled cooking spray

250 g (9 oz) dried tagliatelle

16 cherry or baby plum tomatoes

1 red or green chilli

300 g (10½ oz) passata (sieved tomatoes)

salt and freshly ground black pepper

20 g (¾ oz) vegetarian Parmesan shavings, to serve

fresh basil leaves, to garnish

1 Preheat the char-grill pan or grill. Spray the asparagus with the cooking spray and char-grill or grill the spears in batches, until tender.

2 At the same time, put the tagliatelle into the saucepan and cover with plenty of boiling water from the kettle. Cook for 10-12 minutes, or according to the packet instructions, until tender.

3 Slice the tomatoes in half and finely slice the chilli, removing and discarding the seeds.

4 Drain the cooked tagliatelle in the colander. Tip the passata into the hot saucepan and add the tomatoes and chilli. Bring to the boil; then return the tagliatelle to the saucepan and add the asparagus, snipping it into pieces with scissors as you add it. Stir everything together gently and season. Share the pasta between 4 warmed bowls or plates.

5 To serve, sprinkle a quarter of the Parmesan shavings over each portion and garnish with the basil leaves.

Cook's tip Judge how much chilli you need – if it's a large one, half of it may be enough.

Frittata to go

These tasty wedges are perfect for packing up and eating on the go.

ProPoints values per serving	6 ProPoints value
ProPoints values per recipe	25
Serves 4	

At the ready

a large saucepan on the hob

a kettle of boiling water

a food processor with grater attachment

a non-stick frying pan

kitchen scissors

Ingredients

100 g (3½ oz) very small dried pasta
  shapes

1 courgette

4 spring onions

calorie controlled cooking spray

6 eggs

2 tablespoons skimmed milk

2 teaspoons dried mixed herbs

1 roasted red pepper (from a jar, packed
  in brine)

50 g (1¾ oz) reduced fat mature Cheddar
  cheese, grated

salt and freshly ground black pepper

1 Put the pasta shapes into the saucepan and cover with plenty of boiling water from the kettle. Cook for 3-4 minutes, or according to the packet instructions, until just tender.

2 While the pasta is cooking, grate the courgette and spring onions in the food processor. Heat the non-stick frying pan and spray with the cooking spray. Add the courgette and spring onions and cook for 2-3 minutes, stirring often.

3 Drain the pasta, rinse it with cold water to cool quickly and drain it again thoroughly. Add the pasta to the frying pan.

4 Preheat the grill. Beat the eggs and milk together with the dried herbs and season. Pour the egg mixture into the frying pan and cook over a low heat for 4-5 minutes, without stirring, to set the base. Tear up the pepper and arrange the pieces over the surface of the omelette; then sprinkle it with the grated cheese.

5 Put the frying pan under the grill and cook for 4-5 minutes until the surface has set and is golden brown. Serve at once or, for a packed lunch, cool the omelette completely before cutting it into wedges and wrapping them in cling film or greaseproof paper. Chill until needed.

Cook's tip You can use regular-sized pasta shapes, though they will take a few more minutes to cook.

Taking the wedges to work? Use an insulated container and include a small ice pack to keep the food cool and fresh.

"I always eat my pudding with either a teaspoon or a coffee spoon so that I have to eat slowly and can really enjoy the taste."

Julie Reece Weight Watchers member

Snacks, Desserts + Fruit

Toast toppers

What can you have for a snack that takes literally minutes to make – and is inspiring, fresh and full of flavour? Check out these light-bulb ideas.

Pear, Stilton and walnut melt

ProPoints values per serving	7 ProPoints value
ProPoints values per recipe	14
Serves 2	

Preheat the grill, then warm 2 x 44 g Weight Watchers mini plain naan breads for a few moments. Meanwhile, core and slice a large ripe **pear**, and sprinkle the slices with lemon juice. Spread 2 teaspoons of mango chutney on to each naan and arrange the pear on top. Crumble 15 g (½ oz) Stilton cheese over the pear slices on each naan. Sprinkle 1 teaspoon of chopped walnuts over each naan then grill until the cheese starts to melt.

Peanut butter, banana and chocolate toast

ProPoints values per serving	4 ProPoints value
ProPoints values per recipe	9
Serves 2	

Mix 50 g (1¾ oz) low fat soft cheese with 4 teaspoons (20 g) of crunchy peanut butter, then spread on to 2 slices of toasted **Weight Watchers Malted Danish Loaf**. Slice a small **banana** on top of each one and finish with 1 teaspoon (5 g) of grated chocolate per slice.

Peach and plum grills

ProPoints values per serving	3 ProPoints value
ProPoints values per recipe	6
Serves 2	

Preheat the grill. Pit and slice 1 **peach** and 2 **plums**, then grill the pieces on a baking sheet for a few minutes until softened. Toast 2 slices of **Weight Watchers Danish Loaf** and spread each one with 15 g (½ oz) low fat soft cheese. Spread 1 teaspoon of reduced sugar apricot jam on each slice and scatter with the grilled fruit. Sprinkle 1 teaspoon of demerara sugar over each slice and grill for a few moments.

Cottage cheese crunch

ProPoints values per serving	4 ProPoints value
ProPoints values per recipe	9
Serves 2	

Preheat the grill. Split 1 plain or wholemeal bagel in half and lightly toast the cut sides. Top each half with 2 tablespoons of **low fat cottage cheese**. Core and thinly slice 1 **apple**, then arrange an equal number of slices on each bagel half. Top each half with 15 g (½ oz) halved seedless **grapes** and 1 teaspoon of sultanas.

White bean and red pepper dip

A super-speedy dip; great for a light lunch or put it in a sealed tub and take to work.

ProPoints values per serving	**2** ProPoints value
ProPoints values per recipe	8
Serves 4	

At the ready

a sieve
a blender or hand-held blender

Ingredients

410 g can cannellini beans, **in water**
50 g (1¾ oz) roasted red pepper (from a
    jar, packed in brine)
100 g (3½ oz) low fat soft cheese
1 small crushed garlic clove
a few snipped fresh chives **or** parsley
salt and freshly ground black pepper
vegetable crudités, **to serve**

1 Drain the cannellini beans in the sieve then tip them into a blender. Add the roasted red pepper, soft cheese, garlic and a few snipped fresh chives or parsley, reserving some for the garnish, and season then blitz in a blender until smooth.

2 Garnish with snipped chives and sprinkle over some black pepper. Serve with fresh vegetable crudités of your choice.

Cook's tip **Spread on 4 slices of toasted** Weight Watchers Malted Danish Loaf **and serve topped with sliced** cucumber **and cherry** tomatoes **– this increases the** *ProPoints* **values per serving to 3.**

Get-up-and-go granola

Excellent for a crunchy nibble, or to serve for breakfast with milk and fresh fruit, this granola has far less fat and sugar than bought versions.

ProPoints values per serving	**5**
ProPoints values per recipe	**91**
Makes 20 x 40 g (1½ oz) portions	

At the ready

a large non-stick baking sheet (with
    sides) or a Swiss roll tin
a large bowl

Ingredients

calorie controlled cooking spray
100 g (3½ oz) whole hazelnuts
400 g (14 oz) jumbo rolled oats
50 g (1¾ oz) wheat bran
15 g (½ oz) sesame seeds
50 g (1¾ oz) sunflower seeds
100 ml (3½ fl oz) clear honey
50 g (1¾ oz) dried cranberries
50 g (1¾ oz) raisins or sultanas

1 Preheat the oven to Gas Mark 6/200°C/fan oven 180°C. Spray the baking sheet or Swiss roll tin with the cooking spray.

2 Keep a few of the nuts whole and chop the rest roughly. Mix them all in a large bowl with the oats, wheat bran, sesame seeds, sunflower seeds and honey. Tip the mixture on to the baking sheet and spread it out evenly.

3 Bake in the oven for 15 minutes, stirring every 5 minutes, until the mixture is evenly toasted. Cool completely before stirring in the dried fruit. Transfer to a storage jar and keep in a cool place for up to 1 month.

Variation

Try using ready-to-eat dried apricots instead of cranberries, for a change. The **ProPoints** values per serving will be 4.

> **Cook's tip** **Serve a 40 g (1½ oz) portion with 125 ml (4 fl oz) chilled skimmed milk and fresh fruit for 6 *ProPoints* values per serving.**

Fruity flapjack squares

Delicious oaty nibbles that are perfect for a packed lunch or a treat with your cuppa, and unlike a lot of flapjacks these are really moist.

ProPoints values per serving	**3** ProPoints value
ProPoints values per recipe	53
Makes 16 squares	

At the ready

a large saucepan
a 23 cm (9 inch) square shallow cake tin
baking parchment or greaseproof paper
a food processor with grater attachment
kitchen scissors

Ingredients

100 g (3½ oz) low fat spread
4 tablespoons golden syrup
250 g (9 oz) porridge oats
1 eating apple
50 g (1¾ oz) ready-to-eat dried apricots
50 g (1¾ oz) sultanas or raisins
½ tsp ground mixed spice
1 large egg

1   Preheat the oven to Gas Mark 4/180°C/fan oven 160°C. Melt the low fat spread in the large saucepan. Brush a little over the cake tin, then line the base with baking parchment or greaseproof paper.

2   Stir the syrup into the melted spread and add the porridge oats. Quarter the apple; remove its core and grate the flesh in the food processor (or chop finely by hand). Stir the grated apple into the mixture and snip in the apricots with the scissors. Add the sultanas or raisins and mixed spice. Beat the egg; add it to the mixture and stir thoroughly.

3   Tip the mixture into the prepared tin and level the surface. Bake for 15 minutes until firm. Cool in the tin for about 20 minutes, then cut into 16 squares.

> **Cook's tip** Store the flapjacks in an airtight tin, or pack them in freezer wrap or a freezer box and freeze for up to 3 months.
>
> **Time-saving tip** You could melt the low fat spread and golden syrup in a large microwavable bowl for 30-40 seconds on HIGH, before adding the remaining ingredients as in the method above.

Banapple muffins

This is a really easy and fast way to make muffins. Make sure you are super-speedy though, as this recipe will take the full 20 minutes.

ProPoints values per muffin	**2** ProPoints value
ProPoints values per recipe	**28**
Makes 12	

At the ready

12 paper or silicone bun cases
a bun tray
a sieve
a mixing bowl
a saucepan
a measuring jug
a grater

Ingredients

150 g (5½ oz) plain flour
1½ teaspoons baking powder
50 g (1¾ oz) caster sugar
40 g (1½ oz) low fat spread
100 ml (3½ fl oz) skimmed milk
1 egg
1 teaspoon vanilla extract
1 small apple
1 small banana

1 Preheat the oven to Gas Mark 5/190°C/fan oven 170°C. Put 12 paper or silicone bun cases in the bun tray.

2 Sift the flour and baking powder into a mixing bowl and stir in the caster sugar.

3 Melt the low fat spread in the saucepan and pour it into the jug. Beat in the milk, egg and vanilla extract. Add the mixture to the dry ingredients, grating in the apple. Mash the banana and add it to the mixing bowl, stirring until just combined. Do not over-mix.

4 Spoon the mixture into the paper cases and transfer the tray to the oven. Bake for 15-18 minutes until risen and golden. Cool the muffins on a wire rack.

Variation

For a different taste add ½ teaspoon ground mixed spice or ground cinnamon to the dry ingredients.

Cook's tip **Always use proper cook's measuring spoons for accuracy and level off dry ingredients (such as baking powder) with a knife.**

Quickie fruit crumble

Serve this clever fruit crumble for pudding or you could even try it for breakfast.

ProPoints values per serving	**4** ProPoints value
ProPoints values per recipe	15
Serves 4	

At the ready

a saucepan

a potato peeler

a fine grater

a small saucepan

4 ramekins or heatproof dishes

Ingredients

8 plums

100 ml (3½ fl oz) unsweetened apple juice

1 large orange

a pinch of ground cinnamon or mixed spice

25 g (1 oz) low fat spread

75 g (2¾ oz) low sugar muesli

2 teaspoons demerara sugar

4 tablespoons low fat plain yogurt

1 Pit and slice the plums. Put them in the saucepan with the apple juice, a strip of orange zest (use the potato peeler) and the cinnamon or mixed spice. Simmer gently for 8-10 minutes, until tender.

2 Meanwhile, finely grate 1 teaspoon of zest from the orange. Peel the orange with a sharp, serrated knife, removing all the pith; then cut the flesh into segments and set them aside. Put the zest into the small saucepan with the low fat spread and heat until melted. Remove from the heat and stir in the muesli.

3 Stir the orange segments into the plum mixture; remove the strip of zest and share the fruit between the ramekins or heatproof dishes.

4 Preheat the grill. Spoon the muesli mixture on top of the fruit and sprinkle each portion with ½ teaspoon demerara sugar. Grill for 2-3 minutes. Serve each ramekin with 1 tablespoon of low fat plain yogurt.

Variation

For a change, use 2 eating **apples**, cooked until tender, mixed with 100 g (3½ oz) sliced **strawberries** and the orange, as before, for 4 **ProPoints** values per serving.

Fresh fruit skewers with hot chocolate drizzle

Make fresh fruit into more of a treat by serving it on skewers and drizzling them with a delicious hot chocolate sauce.

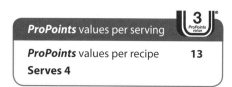

ProPoints values per serving	**3** ProPoints value
ProPoints values per recipe	**13**
Serves 4	

At the ready

8 bamboo sticks
a small saucepan

Ingredients

8 strawberries
2 bananas
2 kiwi fruit
1 large ripe mango

For the chocolate sauce

50 g (1¾ oz) plain chocolate
1 tablespoon cocoa powder
1 tablespoon cornflour
200 ml (7 fl oz) skimmed milk

1 First prepare the fruit. Halve the strawberries, if large; peel and chop the bananas; peel and slice the kiwi fruit; peel, stone and slice the mango. Thread the fruit on to the bamboo sticks, alternating the pieces.

2 To make the sauce, break the chocolate into pieces and put them in the saucepan with the cocoa powder, cornflour and milk. Heat gently, stirring constantly, until smooth and thickened.

3 Serve 2 skewers per person, drizzled with an equal amount of chocolate sauce.

Cook's tip Be adventurous and use whatever zero **ProPoints** value fruits you like.

For a touch of spice Give a subtle kick to the chocolate sauce by adding a pinch of chilli powder.

Light-as-air lemon soufflé omelettes

Soufflé omelettes are simple and quick to cook, yet look and taste amazing.

ProPoints values per serving	2 ProPoints value
ProPoints values per recipe	4
Serves 2	

At the ready

a fine grater
a large mixing bowl
a hand-held electric whisk
a non-stick frying pan

Ingredients

1 lemon
4 egg whites
15 g (½ oz) caster sugar
calorie controlled cooking spray
2 teaspoons icing sugar

1 Finely grate the zest from the lemon. Whisk the egg whites in the bowl using the hand-held electric whisk, until they hold their shape. Gradually add the sugar, whisking well until the egg whites are stiff and glossy. Whisk in the lemon zest.

2 Preheat the grill, warming 2 serving plates under it. Heat the non-stick frying pan on the hob and spray with the cooking spray. Add half the whisked egg white, spreading it to cover the surface of the pan, and cook over a low heat until the base has set – about 2 minutes. Transfer to the grill to set the surface.

3 Slide the omelette on to a warmed plate and cook the second one in the same way. Fold the omelettes and serve dusted with icing sugar. Slice the lemon into wedges for squeezing juice over the top.

Variation

You could also fill omelettes with warm sliced **strawberries** and **blueberries** without adding extra **ProPoints** values.

Cook's tip **You can now buy free-range pasteurised liquid egg white from many supermarkets. Look for it in the chilled cabinet. It will keep for a week in the fridge once opened.**

Why not enjoy one for breakfast? **These omelettes are a great way to kick-start your day – try filling one with sliced fresh fruit.**

Remember **Any trace of grease (including egg yolk) in the bowl or on the beaters will prevent the egg whites from whisking.**

Hot raspberry and mango meringues

This simple but stunning dessert is just the thing when you want a little something special to round off your meal.

ProPoints values per serving	
ProPoints values per recipe	3
Serves 4	

At the ready
4 ramekins or heatproof dishes
a baking sheet
a mixing bowl
an electric whisk

Ingredients
2 medium-sized ripe mangos
250 g (9 oz) raspberries**, thawed if frozen**
2 egg whites
25 g (1 oz) caster sugar

1 Preheat the oven to Gas Mark 5/190°C/fan oven 170°C. Peel, stone and chop the mangos; mix them with the raspberries. Share the fruit between the ramekins or heatproof dishes and place them on the baking sheet.

2 Whisk the egg whites in the mixing bowl until they hold their shape; then whisk in the sugar until stiff and glossy. Share between the dishes and bake for 6-7 minutes until golden brown. Serve immediately.

> **Cook's tip** This type of meringue stays soft and marshmallowy, so don't expect it to dry into a hard, crisp shell.
>
> **Remember** Always use a scrupulously clean bowl and beaters when whisking egg whites – any trace of grease (including egg yolk) will prevent them from increasing in volume.